A Ribbon Bouquet

A Guide To French Ribbon Flowers
and Silk Ribbon Embroidery

Kathy Pace

Pace
Publishing

©1995 Kathy Pace

Photographs, designed by Kathy Pace and taken by
Borg Anderson and Associates
Alan Blakely Photography
Gooseberry Hill
Snelsens Photography

Illustrations by Kathy Pace
Digitized by Niche Associates

First Editing and production by Amber Sargent
Editing Assistant Sandy Jaussi
Technical editing and design by Elizabeth Lane, and Shawn Hsu

Published by Pace Publishing
1881 Old Lincoln Hwy. Coalville, Utah 84017
ISBN 1-887820-00-0

Library of Congress Cataloging-in-Publication Data

Pace, Kathy
A Ribbon Bouquet: A Guide To French Ribbon Flowers and Silk Ribbon Embroidery/by
Kathy Pace; [illustrations by Kathy Pace]. --1st ed. ISBN 1-887820-00-0
1. Ribbon Work
2. Ribbon Flowers
3. Silk Ribbon Embroidery - Patterns

Printed in Salt Lake City
First Edition

Table Of Contents

Acknowledgements 4
Introduction 5

HOW TO USE THIS BOOK 6

Reminiscing About Ribbons 8
Ribbon Care 12

French Ribbon Grandeur

Flower Bouquet 14
    Daisy 17
    Iris 17
    Carnation 18
    Lily 19
    Moss Rose 20
    Morning Glory 20
    Sweet Pea 21

Scattered Flower Collars . .25
    Pansy 26
    Rose 27
    Sunflower 28

Letha's Lilacs 33

Rose & Ivy Spray 37

Victorian Ribbon Jewelry . .41
    Mum 42

Embellished Accessories . .55

Blossoms On Blouses 62

Portrait of Paradise 67

Needlework Boxes 70
    Ribbon Berries 74

Spring Flower Collection . .78
    Daffodil 79
    Tulips 80
    Jonquil 80

A Garden of Flowers 81
    Impatiens 82
    Cocarde 82

GLOSSARY OF SILK
   RIBBON STITCHES . . .84

STEMS AND LEAVES . . .90

French Ribbon Charts 93

Bibliography 94

About the Author 95

Acknowledgements

I would like to give my warmest thanks to all of our sewing friends whose interests in my designs have enabled me to continue in this interesting and wonderful pursuit.

Thanks to my good friend Sharon Pilcher, for encouraging me to write my first book. A special thanks to my sewing ladies who make many beautiful samples for us: Lareen, Jenny, Linda, Jude and Judy. I would also like to mention my gratitude to Elizabeth Lane and Shawn Hsu who both spent many long hours designing this book.

I owe my mother, Billie, many thanks for devoting her boundless energy to helping me so much. Dennis and I really appreciate her help at the trade shows. She is irreplaceable. I truly feel fortunate when I get to spend time with such a remarkable woman.

My thanks goes to my husband Dennis for the many long hours he spends managing the company's many obligations, and for his added personal help and support. I thank Amber, my daughter, who has done everything from researching and typing the manuscript through the final publication of this book. It would not have happened without her help. It was so fun to giggle and work with someone I love so much.

I am grateful to my Heavenly Father for his blessings and love.

Kathy Pace

1995

Introduction

The very first silk ribbon embroidery I saw was exquisite, delicate and beautiful. It was a tiny broach with pastel flowers that looked like miniatures made of some kind of magical soft substance. It took me a long time to get enough courage to put the ribbon into a needle and try it. To my delight, it was easy, fast and rewarding, because with just a few simple stitches and the natural beauty of the silk ribbon, a wonderful flower spray could be created.

In no time at all, I didn't want to do anything else. I embroidered on everything in sight: shoes, clothes, accessories and crafts. During this delightful time of experimenting with silk flowers, I learned how to make a rose out of French wired ribbon. It was overwhelming to think of the possibilities of blending wired ribbon flowers with the delicate silk flowers on clothing.

I continued working with ribbon and soon developed several different types of wired flowers. The narrow size 5, or 7/8", wide ribbon soon became my favorite. It is possible to make small but very detailed flowers with this ribbon. Flowers made with the wider size 9, or 1 $\frac{1}{2}$", ribbons are larger and make a more colorful impact when they are placed on a project. Sometimes this is exactly what is needed. Within one year, we produced fourteen different patterns that feature a combination of silk ribbon

embroidery and French wired ribbon flowers. When we showed the various garments and patterns at retail shows, the comment heard most often was, "They are gorgeous! Do you have all of these techniques in a book so I can learn how to do them?" Not every one wanted to make the exact dress or vest in the pattern, but they wanted to know how to do the ribbon work. It seemed like a great idea to combine the ideas into one bound volume.

The patterns for most of the actual clothing and other projects are available separately if you wish to duplicate our designs; the rose symbol (shown here) and a stock number are on the photo captions when the item is a Gooseberry Hill pattern. This book is written to instruct the beginner in ribbon work. You will learn how to make a wonderful assortment of silk and wired flowers that can be applied to many types of clothing and accessories. It contains diagrams for several small projects and a traceable fold out section for larger diagrams.

You'll find ideas for using the ribbon flowers on many projects. Richly colored photos are usually my favorite part of books and magazines, so it was my desire to entice the eye by including plenty of them in this book. It was a pleasure to put together this guide, and I truly hope you enjoy it.

How To Use This Book

Dear Reader,

You are about to discover an easy, beautiful way to embellish practically anything with ribbons. If you haven't ever made a ribbon flower, try the rose first. Use one yard of French ribbon in any width, and you will see why we love them so much!

To avoid repeating basic instructions several times, you will often be referred to the Table of Contents to find specific directions and French ribbon flower instructions. In each project you will find that the French ribbon flowers will be listed with initial capital letters such as Wired Ribbon Rose. To make this flower you will need to refer to the Table of Contents under 'Rose' to see where the instructions are found. I will simply say French ribbon throughout this book whenever I am referring to the French shaded wired ribbon. All of the flowers and leaves look their best in the shaded ribbons. Instructions will say solid color ribbon if it is needed.

French ribbons are always size 5, or 7/8", width unless another size is mentioned.

Sometimes there is also listed a ribbon color number listed, such as #23 and #19. The numbers are the French color numbers. You can see which ones they are by referring to the color picture of the project or the French ribbon chart.

When the name of a stem or leaf is given, we capitalize it to show that it is a specific type, such as Gathered Center leaf. Detailed instructions can be found in the Stem and Leaf chapter of the book.

All of the silk ribbon stitch names are in all capitals, such as CORAL stitch. Their instructions are found in the Silk Ribbon Glossary. One strand of Flower Thread, a product of DMC, is like one strand of regular embroidery floss. It is a fine cotton thread that is nice for dainty stems.

Whenever I say glue, I am referring to Beacon's Fabri Tac™ glue. This glue is washable and does not bleed through the French ribbons when used sparingly.

I always like to keep a disappearing pen handy for tracing ribbon patterns and project designs. I prefer the type that disappears with time and not water so I do not have to get my project wet. The drawback to this type of pen is that lines sometimes disappear before you are ready to use them, especially in humid climates. I always check my project at the end of the day to see if lines need to be re-marked. I have also found in traveling that lines disappear from projects stored in plastic bags.

Hats from the 1920's

Silk ribbon was crimped and pleated to trim this pink silk baby bonnet. A few silk rosettes added to any old bonnet will make a frameable treasure. From a time of leisure and beauty come the boudoir caps. These were worn by women of the day who radiated elegance and beauty. The first one is trimmed with narrow lace and large ribbon rosettes. Next is a crochet cap with pink ribbon inserts. The bandeau is made with alternating rows of English netting, crimped silk ribbon and a dainty flower trim. A boudoir cap made of shirrred English netting and hem-stitched ribbon flounces is shown on the upper right.

Reminiscing About Ribbons

Producing ribbons for wearable embellishments is an art that dates back to the middle of the fourteenth century.

These ladies in ribbon decorated hats are from an early French fashion print. It was sent as a gift from the author's sister, Shari Kunovsky, who lived in South Africa.

The early art of ribbon embellishment began in France when women wove silk into ribbons on little hand looms. Rows of ribbon were used as trimming for wide borders on sweeping skirts and cuff bands, fancy sleeve scallops and collars. The sleeves of noble women's robes became larger and more intricately decorated toward the end of the fifteenth century, with multiple bows, flowerettes and loops. The French became experts at making beautiful ribbons that were the envy of Europe.

In the late 1600's many Huguenots left France and fled to England to practice their Protestant religion. Among them were numbers of skilled ribbon weavers who brought their expertise to the English cottage industry. Ribbon manufacturers in France, Germany, Austria, England and Switzerland began to compete with each other to produce beautifully colored ribbons which were in demand all over Europe. Coventry became the most important center for production of fancy goods in England, while Lyon and St. Etienne of France lead the industry on the continent.[1]

In England, before the arrival of steam powered engines to work the ribbon looms, the weaving was completed by "out workers" who took the silk home and wove the ribbons in a room called the top shop. These were often connected to the house of the master weaver, or the "first hand", who would oversee and inspect the work. When factories started to rise up in the larger cities and water was available they began to manufacture ribbons with steam power. Some master weavers also brought steam to their top shops. This helped to make an efficient cottage ribbon industry that lasted for many years.

In 1681 Thomas Baskerville of Dunstable, Bedfordshire, noted that some people of his village were weaving rustic straw hats.

*A bandeau and boudoir
cap from Franklin Simon's 1923 catalogue.*

Seven years later 14,000 people in Bedfordshire and two neighboring counties were making a living weaving and selling straw shepherdess hats. This simple hat enjoyed immense popularity up through the 1770's. The fashion spread across the English Channel and when the French decorated the English hats with their "savoir faire" the millinery industry was born.[2]

Hats of one shape or another have been a fun and fanciful accessory ever since. The milliner's demand for new and unusual ribbons for their hats soon inspired the creation of many beautiful ribbons. Weavers learned to combine gold and silver threads with the silk threads, which produced stunning and costly ribbons for dress making and millinery uses.[3]

The Frenchmen made artificial flowers and cocardes, which are fancy feather-like round or plumed ribbon decorations. They developed intricate ways of knotting, ruching, folding and ruffling the ribbons to achieve breath taking bows for corsages and sashes. Often a ruffled bow trimming the under brim of a hat would require 10 yards of ribbon. They made rosettes, pom poms, berries and every kind of flower imaginable.

Even the humble hat band had developed into an ingenious folded, roughed, woven and multi-layered affair. Ribbons could be manipulated into the shape of a bird, dragonfly or exotic flower by the skilled hands of masters in the crafts of ribbon work. Ribbon manufactures wove the ribbons in various gradations of one or two colors to help achieve the lifelike appearance of flowers and leaves. These are called omber for the French word "shaded." Because there were no wires in the edges until after World War II, the ribbons were hand gathered, stitched and glued on the edges to achieve the desired effects.

During the Rococo era, 1750 to 1780, dress makers for the French nobility made flower blossoms, sprays and nosegay out of omber ribbons to trim elaborate court dresses. Court trains and shoulder sashes were also embroidered with delicately narrow silk ribbons. Today omber wired ribbons are still manufactured in a handful of French mills. There is a ribbon museum in St. Etienne, France that has a nice collection of early ribbons and manufacturing pieces.

Men wore caps at home from the end of the 1500's until the late 1800's. They were often made of silk, velvet or wool. Men's caps from the 1600's were sometimes embroidered or quilted. Although they were not just for wearing to bed, the title "night caps" came to mean any informal hat that was worn at home.

Women followed the trend and soon began wearing little round caps made of ruche ribbon, flowery rosettes, and quantities of lace. By the 1870's women no longer wore ribbon decorated hats all day while at home, but they sometimes indulged themselves by wearing fancy boudoir caps to breakfast or tea.[4] Later, during the Flapper Era, a wide head band called a bandeau made of frail netting, silk ribbons and dainty trimmings was popular not only for a lingerie item, but also found its way out for the evening as a dress up accessory.

Joseph Marie Jacquard introduced a loom in 1801 which produced Jacquard ribbon. These ribbon creations would soon rival the beauty of hand embroidered ribbons. Jacquard's loom was capable of the most detailed work ever seen. Even photographs and engravings of buildings or scenes were being produced on ribbon. Souvenir ribbons were often made for special exhibitions and events with this loom.[5]

Dimensional flower making was somewhat easier when wire-edged ribbons were introduced. The extra support of the wires helped the finished creations to hold their shape.

In 1860 the East India Company brought dainty Chinese silk ribbons to Europe. The Victorian ladies loved embroidery and tried their skills on children's dresses and coats, their own gowns, even picture frames and fireplace screens.[6] The French had been embroidering on court dresses for some time, and the delicate art was introduced to the English through the royal court.

Our ribbon flowers and nosegay are so appealing because they are reminiscent of these Victorian decorations. They take us back to a time when fancifully decorated crazy quilts had a lifetime worth of stitches in each one. The quantity of hand work and beautiful creations that a woman displayed in her home were a reflection of her husband's ability to provide domestic help and thus give her more leisure time. Some crazy quilts even have ribbon flowers stitched onto the center of the pieces.

Silk embroidery has been popular in China for centuries. The early Chinese described the gossamer strand of pale silk by naming it after the clouds. During the Han Dynasty, 206 BC to AD 220, they used these "cloud bands" to decorate the borders of carpets with dainty Lily flowers. Some early ribbon work in English museums dates back to the mid 1700's, but silk embroidery's real popularity was born during the Victorian era.

Unfortunately, there are not many surviving pieces of old American ribbon work to be found. Dealers in vintage clothing say ribbons were often too fragile to last through the life of the garment, and were sometimes replaced even while the clothes were still in fashion to extend their use. I have seen a couple of antique examples of ribbon work used to make or decorate different items, some of which are pictured here. I once saw a small ribbon embroidered tablecloth in a box of linens at an auction in Seattle, but I missed it! It had violets and yellow forming a pretty wreath in the center.

One Christmas after I had amassed a ribbon collection that was taking over my sewing room, Dennis gave me a fabulous antique ribbon cabinet! It is made of wood and has glass sides that open to display wooden racks that hold the ribbon rolls. It will hold about 330 assorted rolls of ribbon. The French rolls fit perfectly, just as though they have found their true home! It is fun to display some of my antique ribbon in it, too, tied in rolls with dainty silk rosettes. It was made by the Exhibition Show Case Co. Erie, PA, November 17, 1889. (See photo on page 31)

My husband Dennis and I collect dolls. We especially look for the bisque ones made before the turn of the century. I have found a few nice ribbon bonnets that we put on the dolls. The large one is unusual because it is made from silk on a wire frame. Yards of

These antique dolls in their old ribbon bonnets are from the author's collection.

wide brown ribbon have been gathered onto the wire form by using casings on the ribbons edges, and multi looped bows decorate the top and back. The tiny flowered cap with huge tan colored ties is made with a very wide silk ribbon that is shirred in parallel rows across the top. Velvet flowers and a delicate greenery trim complete this doll-sized treasure. A black lace night cap with looped ribbons on top seems to stay on without ties. It has a strap that goes around the back of the neck, under the hair. One little doll wears a pretty flower garland wreath made with wired metallic ribbons, and little buds which are wrapped with a metal netting. A little antique souvenir doll from Belgium has beautiful embroidered ribbon trimmings and a nice example of jacquard ribbon for the apron.

Ribbon Care

*M*ost stitchers want
to know if embellished
clothing can be washed. The silk ribbons are
delicate, but they can be machine washed gently
in cool water, and then the garment can be line dried. It
is always a good idea to test your ribbon and fabric for color
fastness. The French ribbons are acetate, which simulates the
look of silk, and is easily flattened for the beautiful
embroidered look on clothing and decorator items. Acetate
has a low melting point, so care must be taken when pressing.
I always recommend pressing the embellished areas from the
wrong side using a low temperature. Iron gently, with padding
underneath the embellishments.

*Repeated washings soften the French ribbons and create a
few added wrinkles to the flower, which make them look like
real pressed dried flowers. Sometimes appliqued flowers that
are machine washed seem to shrink away from the stitches
holding them, but some gentle smoothing will make them
look as good as new.

The use of Fabri Tac glue will save a considerable
amount of time with wired ribbon work. Do not use it on
polyester wired ribbons. Stitch them on by hand with
matching thread. Fabri Tac makes a watery stain on polyester
ribbons. Fabri Tac glue is useful when securing the ends of silk
ribbon to the wrong side of some surfaces, such as lace, knits or sheer
fabrics in the place of a knot. This glue is machine washable, but do not
use it on garments that will be dry cleaned.

*The French ribbon companies do not recommend washing their ribbons.
Gooseberry Hill will not take responsibility for any product damage.
Remember to always follow manufacturers' instructions for cleaning clothing.

French Ribbon Grandeur

Exquisite Projects With Ribbon Embellishments

Wired Ribbon Flower Bouquet

The kiss of the sun for pardon,

The song of the birds for mirth,

One is nearer God's heart in a garden

Than anywhere else on earth.

Dorothy Frances Gurney (1858-1932)

Flowers have a beauty and a purity that come to us with love, unchanged from the Creator's hand. Is it because we sense their untainted perfection that we depend upon flowers to help us speak our most poignant feelings; those that words alone can not express? Our love, sorrow, sympathy, and our very best wishes of every kind are better communicated by a gift of flowers.

Although these ribbon flowers are imperfect likenesses, there is joy to be found in creating, giving and wearing them. It is an expression of our gratitude and appreciation for the beauties of the earth.

This is the premier showing of our French wired ribbon flower bouquet. We are proud to introduce the iris, lily, carnation and daisy wired ribbon flowers for the first time. All of the other flowers in the bouquet are found either in this chapter or elsewhere in the book. To find their instructions easily, look in the Table of Contents.

French wired ribbon flowers continue to increase in popularity because they express an element of beauty that everyone can appreciate. The most exciting thing about creating wired ribbon flowers is they are quick and easy. With a little bit of condensing, this bouquet would look glorious on the back of a jacket. Picture the bouquet full sized in brilliant colors on a quilt or pillow.

Flower Bouquet

Supply List
As shown on cover. Finished size 20" by 20"

One 12" doily or 3 different kinds of lace
scraps, appliques or yardage

For Rose: 1⅓ yd French ribbon #23
10" French ribbon #18
Daisy: 3/4 yd white French ribbon
1/8 yd yellow cotton fabric for yo yo
Iris: 1/2 yd French ribbon #22
1/2 yd Silk ribbon mauve #163
Pansy: 3/4 yd French ribbon #22
Carnation: 1 yd French ribbon #251
Lily: 1 yd French ribbon #212
Mum: 1 yd French ribbon white
Moss Rose: 1 yd French ribbon #251
Impatiens: 1/3 yd French ribbon #212
Tulips: 1 yd French ribbon #254
Morning Glory: 1 yd French ribbon #218
Sweet Peas: 1 yd French ribbon #22

2/3 yd French ribbon #186
4⅔ yds French ribbon #19
1 yd French ribbon #34

Flower Thread pale green #2503
Flower Thread medium green #2320

1 yd fabric for back ground

Purchased flower stamens

Glue

Bow: 1 yd of 2" wide green sheer ribbon
1 yd light weight iron-on interfacing

4MM silk ribbon in the following amounts:
Fern: 7 yds Dk. green #21
8 yds moss green: #72
6 yds deep green #171
Stems 3 yds Med. green #32

1. To begin the project, select a medium to heavy weight background fabric. We used a satin jacquard from Land of Lace, which we dyed ecru. Next iron a light weight interfacing on the back.

2. Draw ferns in place using the full sized pattern from the fold out section and a disappearing pen.

3. Select lace motifs, doilies or lace yardage scraps and place between and over fern markings. We used an antique collar and bits of old laces. It is all right if they overlap ferns slightly. Use a small amount of glue to tack lace to the fabric. If you cannot see through lace pieces re-draw fern markings on top of the lace. Tuck raw ends under another piece of lace, or trim them so raw edges are down by the stem area, and they will be covered with leaves or stems.

4. Stitch the ferns with silk ribbon using the JAPANESE ribbon stitch. We used color numbers 21, 72 and 171 to achieve a shaded look. Simply stitch outward from the main stems, with two JAPANESE ribbon stitches that are 3/8" long, with pairs of stitches about 1/4" apart. When you run out of ribbon in your needle, change colors. Ferns also look nice stitched in one color.

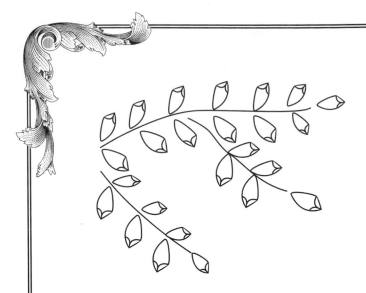

5. Make all of the wired ribbon flowers. There are one each of the following: Wired ribbon Rose and bud, Daisy, Iris, Pansy, Carnation, Lily and Mum. There are two each of: Moss Rose, Impatiens and Tulip. Make the Morning Glories and Sweet Peas as instructed.

6. Make two Wired Bulb leaves with 18" pieces of French ribbon #19, sewn so the dark edge is out, and two with the light edge out. Make two more Wired Bulb leaves using 21" pieces of the same color ribbon with the dark edge out. Stack them so they overlap raw ends as shown with seams on the bottom. Bend the leaves slightly to make a fan shape. Lightly glue on the seam and outer edges to hold leaves in place. Turn under the raw ends on the top leaf.

7. Make Rolled Ribbon Stems for some of the flowers in the following lengths from French ribbon and glue them in place:
Daisy 12" of color #34
Mum 12" of color #34
Lily 14" of color #186
Tulips 13" and 15" of color #19
Iris 16" of color #19

8. Stitch a CORAL stitch stem for the rose using 7MM #72 ribbon.

9. Make STRAIGHT stitch stems with medium green silk ribbon going from behind the Lily and Mum to the Moss Roses and Impatiens.

10. Glue the pansy in place, then make a COUCHED stem using 4MM silk ribbon in medium green.

11. Make two Gathered Center leaves for the daisy with French ribbon #186 and two Folded leaves for the rose using French ribbon #18.

12. Glue the remaining leaves and flowers in place. Tie a bow in the wide ribbon and glue or tack it in place.

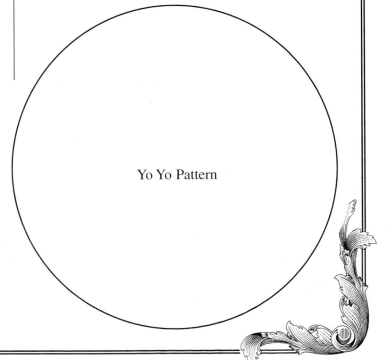

Yo Yo Pattern

Daisy

Supply List for one Daisy
3/4 yd white French ribbon
1/8 yd pale yellow fabric
for yo yo center

A. Cut 27" of French ribbon. Make a crease 1/2" from one end, then make creases every 2" the rest of the length of the ribbon. Unfold it.

B. On the sewing machine, baste along one edge, stitching up to the other edge and back down at each fold. (Sunflower is made by basting along the darker edge.)

C. Pull up the thread to gather the ribbon, and fold the gathered points up on top. Tie off threads. (Sunflower is made by folding the darker gathered points up on top.)

D. Sew the ends' right sides together, and flatten the flower. Glue or stitch it down on top of a yellow yo yo.

E. To make the yo yo, cut one from yo yo pattern. (Sunflower is made by using a brown yo yo.) Fold the outer edge to the wrong side 1/4" and baste all around the outer edge. Pull up thread to gather it tightly, flatten it out, and tie off thread on the back side. Use glue to hold it in place.

Iris

Supply List for one Iris
1/2 yd of 7MM Silk ribbon mauve #163
1/2 yd of French ribbon #22

A. First cut a 16" piece of 1" wide French ribbon. Fold it in half and push out the wires in both of the light edges at the same time.

B. Gather the ribbon while pulling on the two wires.

C. Wrap one wire around one end of the ribbon several times and wrap the remaining wire around the other end of the ribbon several times. Cut off excess wire.

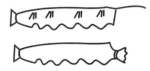

D. Lay the ribbon out flat and make a loop in the center.

E. Make a half twist in the ribbon, $1^1/_2$" from the ends of the ribbons so the gathered edge is on the inside for the lower petals. Cut a $1^1/_2$" piece of ribbon and fold both raw ends under. Stitch or glue it under the upper loop. Take a stitch over the top of the loop with silk ribbon, and another stitch where the ribbon crosses itself. Fold wrapped ends of ribbon under 1/4". Glue or stitch gathered part of ribbon down.

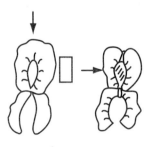

Carnation

Supply List for one Carnation
1 yd of French ribbon #251

A. Cut 1 yard of shaded or plain colored wired ribbon. Pull on the wire in one edge of the ribbon, usually the darker edge if your ribbon is shaded. Pull the wire out for about 7", and then wrap the end of the ribbon with the wire tightly several times. Cut off excess wire.

B. Gather the ribbon along the same wire by pulling out on the wire from the other end of the ribbon, gentle but firmly, until it is as tight as it will gather on the wire. Wrap the second end as you did the first and cut off excess wire.

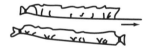

C. Make 1" accordion folds in the gathered edge until only enough ribbon is left to circle completely around the folds. Try to let the upper edge remain ruffly and full while you compact the gathered folds tightly. Either glue or sew the accordion folds together near the gathered edge, then whip stitch or glue the last row of ruffled ribbon around the folded center. Allow the ruffles to stand free of the fabric, just glue or stitch the gathered edge in place. When the flower is smashed with normal wear and use, it will still look pretty. Remove the wire in the light or ruffled edge prior to making the flower if you wish for it to stay fluffy.

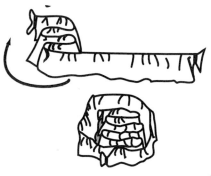

Lily

Supply List for Lily Bloom
1 yd of French ribbon #212
Purchased flower stamens

Lilies can be made with almost any color of ribbon, white, pinks, oranges and lavenders being the most common Lily colors.

A. Cut 5 pieces of French ribbon 7" long. Fold a piece in half and sew by machine from the white edge near the fold to the raw ends of the ribbon in a curved line.

a

B. Fold the corner down twice.

b

C. Open out the petal with seam on the underside. Twist last 1/2" of raw ends together tightly to make a "stem". Set petal

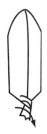

aside and make four more the same way.

D. Gather the petal "stems" into a bouquet. You might want to add some purchased flower stamens to the center of this flower; just glue them in place, or make stamens after the flower is appliqued onto the fabric with straight stitches of flower thread and a FRENCH KNOT or bead at the end. Wrap the stems tightly together with thread and tie off. When you place the flower on a background, hide the stems under a petal, or split them and hide them under two petals. The petals can be bent slightly and arranged to look natural.

Moss Rose

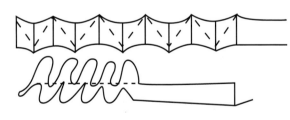

Supply List for one Moss Rose
1/2 yd French ribbon #251
Matching thread

A. Make ten folds, one every inch starting at the end of an 18" piece of French ribbon. Baste a zig zag, starting at the top of the light side and touching the dark edge at the first fold and the light edge at the next fold, etc. Pull the basting thread to form petals and tie off threads at the last fold.

B. Stack and hand tack the dark petals on top of each other so the light petals form a circle.

C. Pull the wire in the light end of the remaining ribbon tail until gathers reach the basting and the tail is 3" long. Then scrunch up the end of the ribbon and wrap the wire

around it several times, near the end, and cut off the excess wire.

D. Hold on to the wrapped end and loosely roll the gathered ribbon tail and tack or glue it on top of the dark petals, gathered side down. Crush it flat to applique it. To applique, come up from under the rose and stitch through the very edge of the ribbon with a tiny stitch every 3/8" to 1/2" around the outside edge and in a few places through the middle of the Rose or use glue.

Morning Glory

Supply List for one Morning Glory Spray
15" French ribbon #19 leaves
1 yd French ribbon #218 for flowers
4MM silk ribbon #21 for stem
 Flower Thread for tendrils #2320

A. Cut a blue and white ribbon as follows for the Morning Glory: 8" for half folded bloom, 7" for fully open bloom, 5" for large bud, and 4" for opening bud. Pull out all of the wires in the white edges.

B. Cut one piece 5" and one piece 4" long and take out the wires in the blue edges.

C. Fold one of the pieces of ribbon in half, and sew across raw ends. Hand bast the edge without wire, then gather it tightly. Tie off and set aside. Repeat for all other pieces.

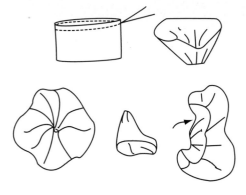

D. Place blossoms so seams are hidden and the gathered edge is underneath the side of the blossom. Place fully open flowers flat, then fold one side of the 8" flower over the center. Pin, then applique or glue as shown in the cover picture.

E. Stitch stem using CORAL stitch. Start down below the bow.

F. Make two Gathered Center leaves from green French ribbon (in the Stem and Leaf chapter).

G. Arrange the four flowers and leaf along the stem in a pleasing way, and glue in place. Stitch curly tendrils with one strand of green Flower Thread. using the STEM stitch.

H. Stitch stem and glue two blue centered buds on the opposite side of the arrangement, then add leaf and tendril as before.

Sweet Pea

*Supply List for one
Sweet Pea Spray*
1 yd French ribbon #22
or color of your choice

10" green French ribbon
for Gathered Center leaves #34

1 yd 4MM silk ribbon #32
pale green Flower Thread #2503

*Sweet Peas shown come on a vine,
so ribbon amounts are enough to
make 7 sweet peas.*

A. Cut seven pieces of French ribbon 5" long. Fold the dark edge of one piece up 1/4", then fold the piece of ribbon in half with the lip on the outside.

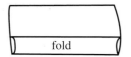

fold

B. With matching thread, hand sew from the raw edge up to the fold and back with long basting stitches next to the lip or edge of the ribbon that is folded up. Pull the thread until it gathers the middle part. Pull both wires in the dark edges at the same time, firmly, and twist them together a couple of times. Cut off the excess wire.

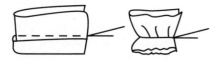

C. Spread out the light edges of the ribbon. Scrunch the ends of the ribbons together and sew through them, or twist them together. Repeat with the other pieces of ribbon.

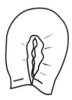

D. When you applique these flowers in place, turn the raw edges under the flower to hide them, or hide their raw ends under another flower. Repeat for other 6 blossoms. Stitch the stems of the flower bouquet with medium green silk ribbon using the CORAL stitch.

E. Make two Gathered Center leaves. Arrange the blossoms along the two stems, which form a fork, so they look pleasing, along with the two leaves, and glue in place.

F. Stitch the curly tendrils with one strand of green Flower Thread using the STEM stitch.

Rose Garland Tree Skirt 🌹 *#201*

Braided organdy and French wired ribbons make up the garland that trails across this Victorian tree skirt. By pulling opposite sides of the shaded wired ribbon, wired ribbon roses will complement each other perfectly. Evergreen sprigs are stitched with embroidery wool. Doilies and lace motifs form a delicate backdrop for the roses.

Classic Collars ✿ #202

We assembled a crazy quilt of deep rich velvets to make the background of this Classic Collar. An assortment of silk ribbon embroidered sprays are used along with beads, lace, buttons, and wired ribbon flowers to adorn this collar.

Lace Flowered Collars 🌹 *#212*

A touch of ribbon elegance will transform your purchased crochet collar from a simple lace accessory to a silk and wired ribbon masterpiece.

Scattered Flower Collars

This is a quick and easy project for the beginner. There are many ways to use this simple ribbon design. It will work gracefully on any shirt with a button front, on a jacket shoulder, ready made vest, or jumper. Any of the collar designs will be pretty on a T-shirt.

If you are going to add flowers to a crochet collar, you will be surprised at how versatile this accessory can be. When looking for a garment to wear with the collar, choose fabrics that do not have large prints that will fight for attention with the ribbon work, like denim, small stripes and plaids, and solid colors that coordinate. The rose collar is the simplest to make, and it looks elegant over a coat type dress or worn with a skirt and blouse. It is equally as fashionable worn over a denim blouse or dress to go out to lunch with the ladies, or on a velvet jacket or dress for an evening at the opera.

The roses that are pictured on the lace collar are made from French ribbon #22, which is gathered on the opposite edge to make the roses on the T-shirt, but any of the many available rose colors will look attractive in this design.

The sunflower collar that is pictured is made from two crochet place mats using a pattern available from Gooseberry Hill. However, the sunflowers look lovely on any purchased collar or T-shirt. Use the Pansy Collar instructions but make sunflowers instead of pansies and eliminate the buds. Make a LAZY DAISY flower with three petals, using 4MM silk ribbon in yellow. Make a brown FRENCH KNOT for the center of the flower. These little sunflowers can be stitched along the stem as desired.

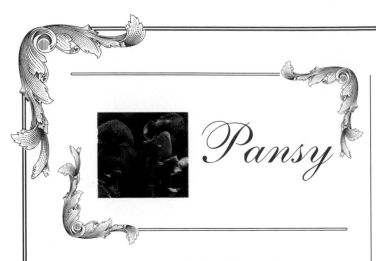

Pansy

Supply List for one Pansy
2/3 yd French ribbon
and matching thread

Or 9" of one color and 15" of
  second color as for
  purple and yellow pansy

5" of green French ribbon #34
for one Gathered Center leaf
For one bud: 5" French ribbon

A. Cut one piece of color #23 French ribbon 9"
long. Fold it in half, and push back on the
ribbon to expose the wires in the light
colored edges. Pull on both of the wires at
the same time.

B. Gather the ribbon on the wires as tight as you
can, and twist the wires to hold the gathers.
Lay the petal out flat. Wrap the wires over
the middle of the ribbon a couple of times,
and straighten the petal out flat again. Cut off
excess wires.

C. Cut three pieces of #23 French ribbon 5"
long. Pull out the wires in the darker edges.
Sew with a basting stitch from the light edge,
across the end, along the dark edge, and
across the other end. Pull the gathering
stitches to form a petal. Tie off the thread.

D. Repeat for other two petals. Layer the petals
on top of the first double petal and each other
as shown to hide the raw ends. (1, 2, 3, 4)
and sew through all layers to hold the petals
together, then flip the top petal down. We
made a different colored flower by gathering
the opposite edges of the ribbon.

Pansy Bud

Cut 5" of French ribbon. Fold both ends down at
a right angle as shown. Fold the ribbon
in half, and in half again. Twist the ends
together, and fold them up 1/4" twice. Hide raw
ends under a Gathered leaf. I usually use the
CORAL stitch for pansy stems.

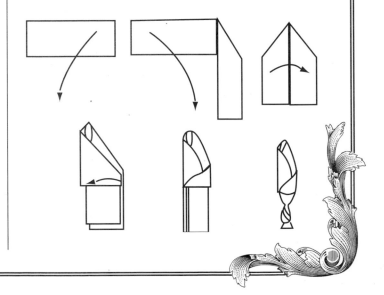

Rose

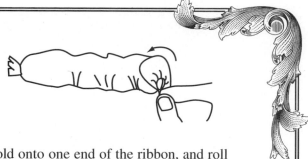

Supply List for one Rose
5" green French wired ribbon for each leaf

1 yd colored French wired ribbon per Rose

For one Rose bud: 12" French ribbon, but you can use any length from 6" to 30".

Use either the Rolled Wired stem, CORAL or COUCHED stem instructions.

A. Gently pull the wire in one edge of the ribbon to gather it for a couple of inches. Wrap the end of the ribbon with the wire.

B. Start at the other end of the ribbon, and pull on the same wire, to gather the ribbon about as tight as it will go. Wrap the end as before. Cut off excess wires. A 36" piece of ribbon should now be about 12" long.

C. Hold onto one end of the ribbon, and roll the ribbon around it to form a rose.

D. The last few rolls should spiral outward so they are about 1/4" from the previous row. See the underside of the rose. Hand stitch the gathered ribbon to the previous row with invisible or matching thread, or use a tiny amount of glue to keep coils in place. Then, glue or applique it in place.

To applique a wired ribbon flower to a project, use pins to hold it in place. You may use invisible thread or matching thread. When working with invisible thread, use a double thread, and a knot in both threads together to keep it from coming unthreaded as you sew. Come up from underneath one edge of the ribbon and take a small stitch down beside the ribbon into your fabric. Repeat this every 1/2" all around the outside edge of the Rose. Then take more stitches through the Rose, tacking down the edges of the inner petals to whichever part of the Rose they rest on, only as needed.

To glue the Rose down, simply fill the coils at the base of the rose with glue and place a bead of glue around the outer edge of the Rose, and press it down in place. Some additional glue might be needed under some parts of the Rose to keep it flat.

Rose Underside

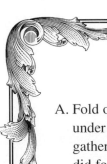

Rose Bud

A. Fold one end of a 12" piece of French ribbon under 1/8" twice. Begin at the other end, and gather the ribbon by pulling on a wire as you did for the rose.

B. Wrap the end of the ribbon with the wire, and cut off the excess. Roll the bud from the wrapped end. Stitch as you did the Rose if desired, and flatten it over sideways so that gathers, stitches, and folded end are hidden underneath. Buds can be glued too.

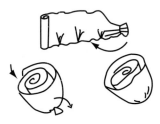

Sunflower

Supply List for one Sunflower
3/4 yd gold French ribbon #11

Small scrap of brown printed cotton Fabric for yo yos

10" French green ribbon #19 for two Folded leaves

Yellow thread

Stem: 10" of 7MM silk ribbon green #21

The sunflower is made the same as the Daisy in the bouquet chapter. The stem is made by stitching down the center of matching 7MM green silk ribbon. Use Folded leaf instructions.

Pansy Crochet Collar

(pictured on page 24)
Directions for Pansy Collar

1. Make two Wired Ribbon Pansies with #29 ribbon, and three with #23 ribbon. Make two Pansy buds with #23 and three Folded leaves. These can be glued onto the shirt or collar, or appliqued on by stitching all around the outer edges using little stitches and matching thread.

2. Thread a needle with 7MM green silk ribbon. Starting about 13" up from one tie end (try on the collar to see where the flower spray should go), sew a running STRAIGHT stitch "stem" that is 1/2" long on top and very short underneath, along the center of the crochet tie. Follow the straight part of the crochet all the way around the back of the collar, and end with a knot or a dab of glue to hold the end of the ribbon to the underside of the collar 13" from the other tie's end. Straighten the ribbon as you stitch, so the stitches lay flat on top.

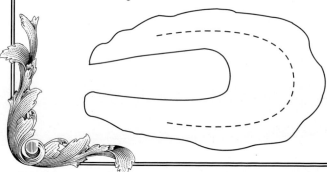

3. Tie a bow in 18" of French ribbon. Fold the ends under 1/4" twice to the wrong side, and wrinkle the tie ends a little. Press it flat between your palms. Place it on the collar, with the knot 5" up from the beginning of the stem.

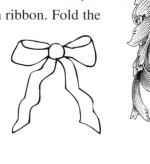

4. Place a pansy just above the bow, and slightly to the right. Place a leaf and bud just above this pansy, and a darker pansy just to the left. Glue or stitch the flowers, leaf, bud and bow in place. Sew a second stem of running STRAIGHT stitches just to the left of the first, going just behind the knot of the bow and up to the higher pansy.

5. Glue the remaining pansies, leaves and bud on the collar as shown, and stitch a silk ribbon PANSY at each place indicated by the X on the Collar illustration. (See the Silk Ribbon Glossary)

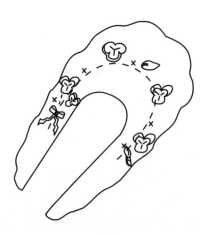

Pansy T-shirt

To make the Pansy T-shirt, use the directions for the Pansy Collar, including ribbon amounts, and arrange the flowers the same way. Use a disappearing pen to mark the stem lines on the front of the T-shirt. Cross the ends of the stem as shown, 8" down from the center front of the shirt. It is a good idea to work in an embroidery hoop. Use iron-on interfacing in the area behind the stitchery to help stabilize the knit. An embroidery hoop with a soft rubber ring works well on knits, so you don't stretch the shirt. We did all of the silk ribbon work first, and then glued on the flowers last so they would not get in the way of the hoop. Continue the collar design around the back of the shirt if desired. When gluing the flowers on, place a layer of saran wrap inside the shirt, so if any glue comes through, it will not glue the shirt together. Use the same stitches and methods described in the collar instructions.

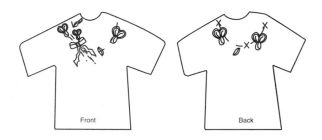

Front   Back

Rose Crochet Collar

(Ties in Front)
Supply List
1 yd French ribbon #18
3 yds of French ribbon #22
5 yds of 7MM silk ribbon green #72
5 yds of 4MM silk ribbon lavender #177

Glue

(pictured on page 24)

Directions for Rose Crochet Collar

1. Make two 30" Wired Ribbon Roses, two 18" Wired Ribbon Roses, one 12" bud, and five Folded leaves.

2. Stitch a running STRAIGHT stitch stem exactly as for the pansy collar. Silk ribbon flowers are mixed in between the Roses. They are made by making two 7MM green #72 leaves with LAZY DAISY stitch and three petals of LAZY DAISY stitch lavender #177, with a lavender FRENCH KNOT center and two FRENCH KNOT buds beside the flower. Stitch silk ribbon flowers at the X mark, then make a bow from 18" of ribbon just as for the pansy collar.

This is the silk ribbon flower

Rose T-shirt

To make a Rose T-shirt, use the same ribbon amounts as for the Rose Crochet Collar.

Mark and stitch stem lines on the T-shirt just as for the Pansy T-shirt, but place Roses where the Pansies are shown.

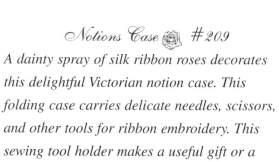

Notions Case 🌹 *#209*

A dainty spray of silk ribbon roses decorates this delightful Victorian notion case. This folding case carries delicate needles, scissors, and other tools for ribbon embroidery. This sewing tool holder makes a useful gift or a pretty addition to your needle work basket.

The author's antique ribbon cabinet.

Lilac Dress  *#211*

Embellish any plain garment with silk ribbon lilacs and wired ribbon bows. Pictured is
Gooseberry Hill's comfortably fashioned casual dress. A Wired Ribbon Rose and leaves on a
lace motif is also an easy embellishment for the bodice.

Letha's Lilacs

One summer, I was planning a special surprise for my friend Letha's birthday. I wanted to create an enchanting ribbon piece that would reflect her charming and elegant style.

In the comfortable parlor of her Victorian home, named the *Lilac Sweet Homestead*, she and two other friends hosted "Occasional Teas." I pictured Letha as the hostess, wearing a country jumper with some kind of flowers decorating the shoulder. This jumper seemed like the perfect outfit for her tea parties.

I asked Letha what her favorite flower was, hoping she would say roses, pansies, or sweet peas or any of the flowers that I already knew how to make from ribbon. When she said "Lilacs, of course!" I smiled and thought to myself, "Oh, no! How am I going to create a lilac?"

I experimented with different techniques and discovered a way to create silk ribbon lilacs. The blossoms are too tiny to be made with French ribbon, so I used Japanese stitches with silk ribbon. The blossoms are made from four stitches that form a circle. French knots represent unopened buds at the top of each blossom spray.

Letha's lilacs looked beautiful in lavender shades on her pale green ticking striped jumper. This pattern is appropriately named after Letha, who inspired it.

This cluster of dainty flowers looks great on a sweatshirt, vest or hat box lid. We have listed the yardage needed to make Letha's lilacs out of the grape and lavender colors. The diagram is in the fold out section and it will look like the small spray on the shoulder of the dress. Follow the yardage amounts to mix and match your own colors.

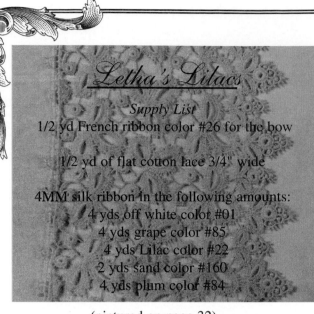

Letha's Lilacs

Supply List
1/2 yd French ribbon color #26 for the bow

1/2 yd of flat cotton lace 3/4" wide

4MM silk ribbon in the following amounts:
4 yds off white color #01
4 yds grape color #85
4 yds Lilac color #22
2 yds sand color #160
4 yds plum color #84

(pictured on page 32)

Directions for Letha's Lilacs

A. Transfer the design areas of the Lilac pattern (in fold-out section) onto the desired area of fabric using a disappearing pen.

B. Tie a bow in the 18" of French ribbon and lace together. Turn the ends of the ribbon under 1/4" twice to the wrong side. Make little bends in the tails of the bow. Draw the location of the bow onto the fabric. Applique it in place after the silk ribbon work is finished, by taking tiny stitches over all the edges of the ribbon and lace.

C. Make FRENCH KNOTS for the top of a Lilac spray. Make flowerlet from four JAPANESE ribbon stitches to fill in the design areas of each Lilac spray. Make stems with STEM stitch.

A close up view of Letha's Lilacs on our Lilac Dress.

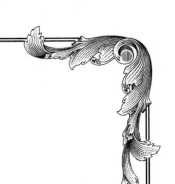

This lilac spray adds a touch of spring to any project and can be made by using a variety of different spring colors to coordinate with your fabrics. For example, monochromatic blues, peaches or mauves. The table cloth stitched by a friend, Janet Blonquist, is bordered with several lilac sprays and has a larger lilac bouquet in the center. French ribbon Folded leaves and Roses can be added to the lilac sprays, as shown.

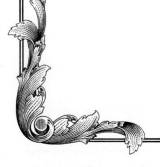

Riding Vest ❦ *#210*

Rose & Ivy Spray

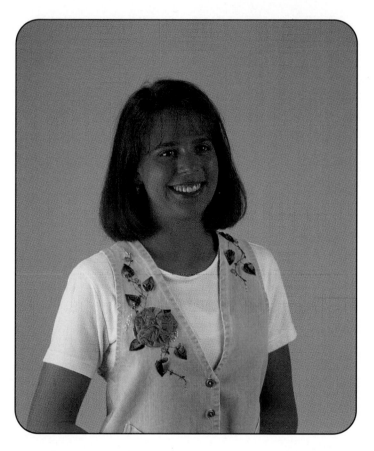

*T*his vest reminds me of a fox hunt complete with English saddles and riding boots. Roses form a surprising but pleasing contrast to the structured plaid fabric. Try making a printed vest with a plain collar and choose ribbons that match the flowers in the print to embellish the collar. The natural combination of roses and ivy leaves decorates a large shoulder or collar area in a short amount of time. Tiny silk CHAIN STITCH ROSES with JAPANESE stitch leaves and buds add charming details as they balance and complete the design.

We have used this design on a jumper. It would also be attractive on a linen jacket or a wool blazer. Decorate an ordinary denim vest with the rose and ivy spray design. Use different colors of ribbon and a variety of beads to make each design unique. Some pretty combinations include plum French ribbon roses with lavender silk roses and peach and yellow French ribbon roses with yellow silk roses. The spray also looks rich with all the ribbon roses in bright Christmas red.

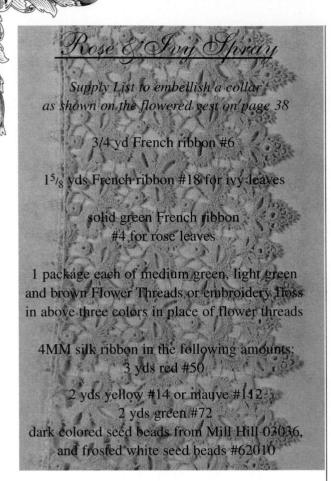

Directions for Rose and Ivy Spray

1. Make Ivy Leaves as shown in Stem and Leaf chapter using the shaded green French ribbon, but cut the lengths as follows: Two leaves from 6" pieces of ribbon, three from 5" pieces of ribbon, and three from 4" pieces of ribbon.

2. Make a Wired Ribbon Rose using 27" of French ribbon.

3. Use a pen that disappears with time so you don't have to use water on your fabric. With the pen, mark where you would like to place the flowers, leaves and stems. A white chalk pencil is nice for dark colors.

4. Make two Folded Leaves from the Stem and Leaf chapter to go next to the Wired Rose. Use solid green French wired ribbon.

5. Stitch the stems for the silk roses with one strand of Flower Thread, or two strands of Med. green floss, using a STEM stitch. The line for silk rose stems is plain. STEM stitch the crossed line the same way in brown for the ivy stems. Use the light Flower Thread or floss to make STRAIGHT stitches to form the babies' breath sprays near the Wired Rose. Sew frosted white seed beads at the ends of the little stems.

6. Make the silk ribbon roses along your stems as desired using the CHAIN STITCH ROSE from the Silk Ribbon Glossary.

7. Make the green leaves with green silk ribbon for silk roses using JAPANESE ribbon stitch.

8. Make the flower buds with two colors of silk ribbon threaded in the needle at the same time using JAPANESE ribbon stitch.

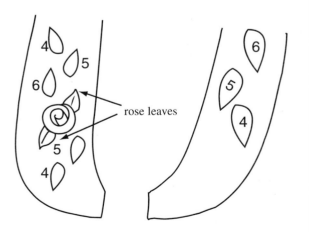

rose leaves

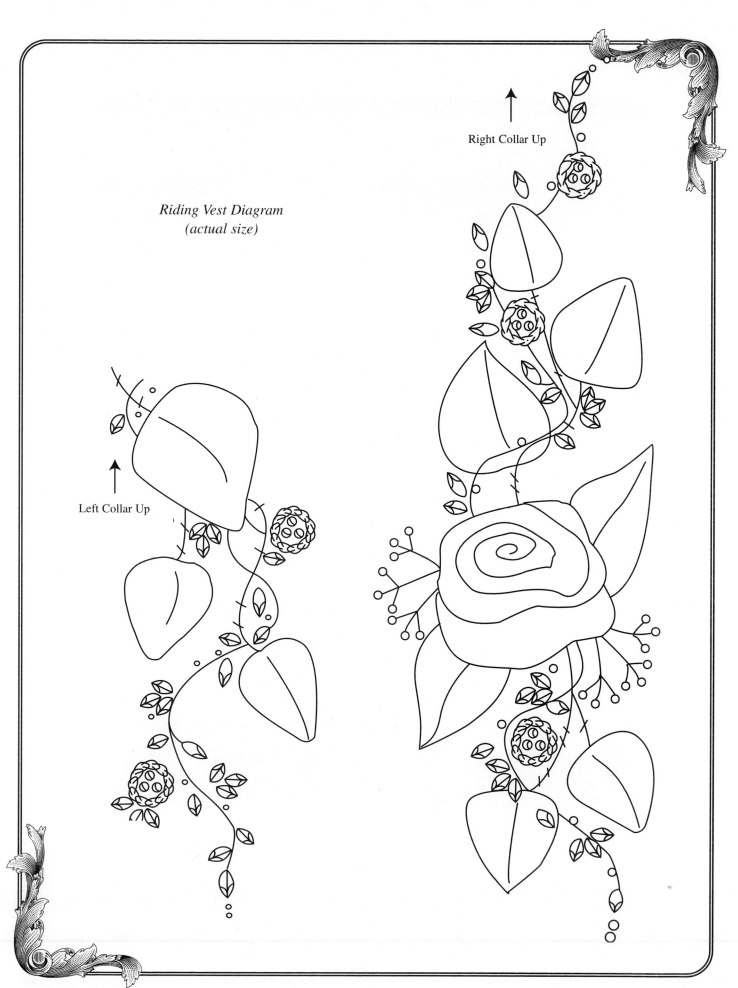

Riding Vest Diagram
(actual size)

Right Collar Up

Left Collar Up

Ribbon Jewelry 🌹 *#205*

Classic silk embroidery earrings, broaches and barrettes are easily made with a few stitches and changeable earring parts. Learn to make a dress or jacket clasp rose combined with delicate lace.

Victorian Ribbon Jewelry

*W*hen I was very young, it was a special treat to go with my mother into her bedroom and browse through her keepsake drawer. There she kept the white heart shaped box that held her wedding ring, her mother's oval locket containing her parents wedding picture, gloves to match all of her purses and shoes, artificial corsages from fancy gowns, and many other intriguing heirlooms. Each momento told a special story. The pretty little treasures in my mother's drawer inspired this collection.

The lacy gloves would be just right to wear in a wedding line and could later be hung from pretty ribbons as a wall decoration.

We have included the instructions for all of the gloves and broaches shown above, along with a delightful collection of earrings, broaches and barrettes from our Ribbon Jewelry pattern. There is a hint of Victoriana in this combination of soft beautiful roses and silk ribbon stitchery.

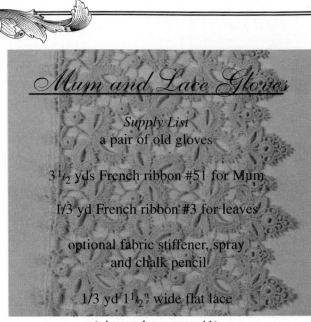

Mum and Lace Gloves

Supply List
a pair of old gloves

3¹/₂ yds French ribbon #51 for Mum

1/3 yd French ribbon #3 for leaves

optional fabric stiffener, spray
and chalk pencil

1/3 yd 1¹/₂" wide flat lace

(pictured on page 41)

Directions for Mum and Lace Gloves

1. Make a Mum using the directions that follow. Make two Folded leaves from French ribbon, and glue or tack the ends of the leaves behind the flower.

2. Use a small piece of ribbon to tie the two gloves together, with one glove slightly higher than the other. Gather one edge of 12" of flat lace, and glue or stitch it to the top glove.

3. Position the Mum and leaves so the leaves cover the raw ends of the lace, and glue or tack the Mum in place. To hang the gloves, tie a bow in 2/3 yd of French ribbon, then tack it to the center of a 1/2 yard piece of ribbon that is folded in half to form a loop. Tie the ends of the loop ribbon in an over hand knot, then secure the knots to the back glove with a few stitches. You might stuff the gloves slightly, or use fabric stiffener spray to give them more body.

Mum

Supply List
3¹/₂ yds French ribbon #51 for
a peach Mum

A. Cut one yard of French ribbon.

B. Fold the ribbon in two inch folds, the entire length of the ribbon. Unfold it. On the machine, sew with a long basting stitch along the darker edge if there is one, stitching up to the other edge and back down at each fold.

C. Pull the bobbin thread to gather the ribbon, and fold the darker or smaller points up on top. Tie off the threads, and coil up the flower, so all the petals show. Either hand sew or glue the coils at the back, making sure to keep raw ends hidden behind the flower.

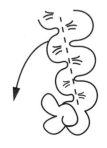

Rose Gloves

Supply List

1 pair crochet gloves
2 yds French ribbon #20

(pictured on page 41)
Directions for Rose Gloves

Make a Wired Ribbon Rose from one yard of French ribbon, and glue or tack it to the glove, being careful to only catch the top layer of the glove in the stitching. If you choose to glue roses onto gloves use a piece of saran wrap inside gloves to prevent glue from closing gloves.

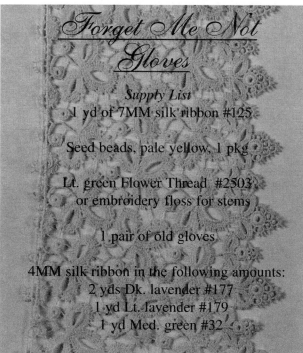

Forget Me Not Gloves

Supply List

1 yd of 7MM silk ribbon #125

Seed beads, pale yellow, 1 pkg

Lt. green Flower Thread #2503
or embroidery floss for stems

1 pair of old gloves

4MM silk ribbon in the following amounts:
2 yds Dk. lavender #177
1 yd Lt. lavender #179
1 yd Med. green #32

(picture on page 41)
Directions for
Forget Me Not Gloves

A little dab of glue will hold the end of the silk ribbon to the underside of the glove, if a knot is too difficult. We used a chalk pencil to draw the stem lines of the back of the gloves.

1. Draw the stem lines on the back of a glove.

Stitch them with a single strand of embroidery floss, or Flower Thread, using a STEM stitch.

2. Using Dk. lavender silk ribbon, stitch the tops of the flowers at the ends of the stems by making two LAZY DAISY stitches. One bud is made with one LAZY DAISY stitch, and a leaf of JAPANESE ribbon stitch into the center of it.

3. Make the lower part of each flower by stitching a JAPANESE ribbon stitch with 7MM blue ribbon. Sew a seed bead in the center of each flower.

4. Make leaves with green ribbon using JAPANESE ribbon stitch.

5. Tie a tiny bow in 1/2 yd of silk ribbon from Lt. lavender silk ribbon. Thread one end of the tie through a needle, and sew three running STRAIGHT stitches, ending with a knot on the back. Repeat for the other tie end. Secure the bow with a drop of glue, or a stitch with regular thread from the wrong side.

Note: This design works on the oval broach or necklace, made from Creative Charms. Trace the design onto a piece of fabric that is large enough to put in an embroidery hoop. After the work is done, Trace the cutting oval on page 47, and center it over the embroidery. Then cut it out, and follow the steps on the charm package for assembly.

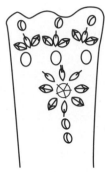

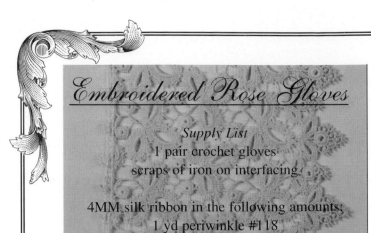

Embroidered Rose Gloves

Supply List
1 pair crochet gloves
scraps of iron on interfacing

4MM silk ribbon in the following amounts;
1 yd periwinkle #118
2 yds green #171
2 yds grape #85

(pictured on page 41)

Directions for Embroidered Rose Gloves

1. Put the glove on your hand to stretch it slightly.

2. Cut a 4" X 3" piece of iron on interfacing, and place it sticky side down inside a glove that is thumb side up. Press for a moment with a warm iron from the thumb side to adhere the interfacing.

3. Make a WOVEN ROSE just above the center flower or in the middle back of the glove. A little dab of glue will hold ends of ribbon when you are finished stitching.

4. Make three buds around the rose with LAZY DAISY stitches, and two FRENCH KNOTS above the last bud, using ribbon of a contrasting color.

5. Make three buds and a FRENCH KNOT by each bud, across the lower edge of the glove. Use the same color ribbon as the rose.

6. Make JAPANESE ribbon stitch leaves on each side of all the buds (except the leaf that is a LAZY DAISY stitch between the two buds that are under the rose), using green ribbon.

7. If desired, gently pull and trim away excess interfacing, leaving only that which is sewn into the flowers. Repeat all steps for other glove.

Embroidered Rose Glove illustration

Broaches or Necklaces

Use a tiny dab of glue to hold the end of the ribbon on the underside of the needlework. Try to keep glue away from areas that will be stitched later. It is helpful to cut out the inner heart or oval on each pattern, and using a disappearing pen, draw the shape in the center of your fabric piece.

This shape acts as a guide to help keep all of the embroidery inside the line. Remember to leave enough fabric around the traced cutting lines on each broach so it can be placed in a hoop. A 10" square of fabric fits in a 6" hoop.

Small Heart Charm

4. Make a WOVEN ROSE using darker mauve ribbon for the inside of the rose, and lighter mauve for the outside. You will tie off the darker mauve on the wrong side before starting the lighter color. Continue the lighter color until the spokes of the circle are full.

Actual size

5. Make two LAZY DAISY buds, using darker mauve ribbon, then make JAPANESE ribbon stitch leaves with dark green ribbon

6. Center the design in the middle of the small heart cutting pattern, then cut it out. It is easier to assemble if you clip the area between the bumps with little 1/4" clips every 1/4".

(pictured on page 41)

Directions For Small Heart Charm

1. Top stitch the lace at an angle across the fabric so the rose will be on the lace.

2. Trace the design onto fabric with a disappearing pen.

3. Stitch stem lines with flower thread or one strand of embroidery floss, using STEM stitch.

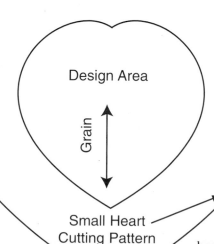

Design Area

Grain

Small Heart
Cutting Pattern

7. Put the charm together as instructed in the package. Glue twist cord around the charm, or twist the silver thread and the 7MM ribbon together by gluing the ends of the thread and ribbon together to the point of the heart. Then wrap the ribbon around the heart. Glue the ends together at the point. Trim off the excess ribbon.

Blue Rose Heart

Supply List
1/6 yd cream linen

A small scrap of iron-on interfacing

1/6 yd each of moss green 1/2" wide sheer
ribbon and Lt. blue sheer ribbon
OR 1/6 yd each of two colors
of 1/2" wide satin ribbon (blue and green)

1/3 yd 1/2" wide flat lace

Blue seed beads #2026

4MM silk ribbon in the following amounts:
1 yd green #171
1 yd Lt. blue #125
1 yd Dk. blue #126

1 pkg Flower Thread #2611 or embroidery floss

1/3 yd small braid trim or ribbon that is 1/8"
wide

A medium Pat and Pam Creative Charm heart

(pictured on page 41)
Directions for Blue Rose Heart

1. Trace the medium heart cutting pattern (on
the following page) onto the linen. Cut one
medium heart tracing pattern from iron-on
interfacing, and center it in back of the large
heart, then iron it on the linen.

2. Weave the two pieces of 6" lace with a blue
and an olive green sheer ribbon. Place them
slightly off center on the right side of the

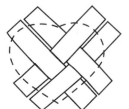

fabric that is interfaced. Use a tiny amount of
glue where they cross each other to hold
them. Baste just inside the outer line, or
cutting pattern, to hold the ends of the ribbon
in place.

3. Mark the location of the flower design with
disappearing pen. Stitch the stem with one
strand of Flower Thread, using STEM stitch.

4. Stitch the WOVEN ROSE, using light blue
ribbon for a FRENCH KNOT at the center,
then weave with light blue ribbon for a few
times around and use darker blue for the
outer rows of weaving. Do two buds of each
color of blue, using LAZY DAISY stitch,
and make two light blue FRENCH KNOTS
at the ends of the design.

5. Make leaves with JAPANESE ribbon stitch,
and the olive green silk ribbon. Cut out the
design on the medium heart cutting line. Clip
the top edge between the bumps, every 1/4"
with 1/4" clips. Assemble as directed on
charm package. Glue braid trim or narrow
ribbon around the outer edge.

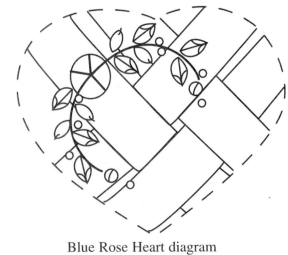

Blue Rose Heart diagram
actual size

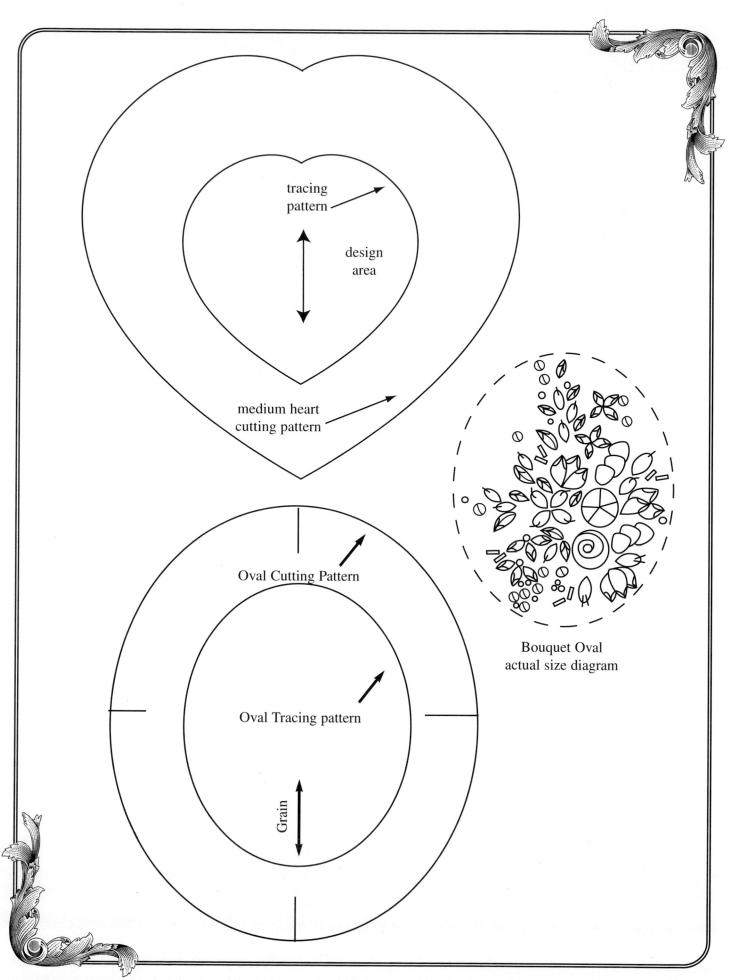

tracing pattern

design area

medium heart cutting pattern

Bouquet Oval
actual size diagram

Oval Cutting Pattern

Oval Tracing pattern

Grain

Bouquet Oval

Supply List

1/4 yd ivory linen

7MM silk ribbon in the following amounts:

1/2 yd mauve #163

1/2 yd Dk. mauve #112

1/2 yd cream #01

4MM silk ribbon in the following amounts:

1 yd green #33

1/2 yd Lt. green #31

1 yd pink #8

1 yd pale yellow #14

1/2 yd cream #01

1/2 yd Lt. blue #125

1 yd Med blue #126

clear seed beads in pink, blue and crystal
cream colored small bugle beads

1 1/2 yds white boucle cord
or small twist cord

medium oval Pat and Pam Creative Charm

a small piece of iron on interfacing

(picture on page 41)

Directions for Bouquet Oval

1. Iron interfacing onto the back of a piece of fabric that is 8" square.

2. Trace the bouquet oval in place on the right side of the linen (diagram on previous page). To embroider, make a WOVEN ROSE, GATHERED ROSE, FREE FORM TWISTED LOOP flower and a JAPANESE FLOWER in the center part first, then fill around them with the smaller sprays of LAZY DAISY, FRENCH KNOTS, JAPANESE stitches and seed beads.

3. When finished, assemble and glue twist cord around the outer edge.

Rose Bud Necklace

Supply List

1/6 yd ivory linen

1/6 yd 1 1/2" wide flat lace

8" of French ribbon #23

1/2 yd #72 silk ribbon 7 MM wide

1 1/2 yds dark red boucle cord
(narrow twist cord)

medium oval from
Pat and Pam Creative Charm

small scrap iron-on interfacing

(picture on page 41)

Directions for Rose Bud Necklace

1. Iron interfacing onto the back of a piece of fabric that is 6" square.

2. Top stitch a piece of lace at a diagonal across the linen.

3. Make a Rose Bud out of 8" of French ribbon, and glue it in the center of the linen.

4. Make a stem for the rose bud with one long stitch of green 7MM ribbon. Take a little stitch over the stem.

5. Make three leaves using 7MM silk ribbon, and LAZY DAISY stitch.

6. Cut out the cutting oval, and assemble the charm. Glue boucle around the outer edge, and use the rest for the necklace.

Flower Garden Heart

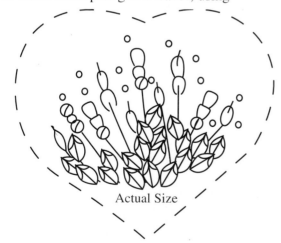

Supply List
1/6 yd green checked fabric

Flower Thread #2369 or embroidery floss

4MM silk ribbon in the following amounts:
1/2 yd periwinkle #118
1/2 yd lavender #22
1/2 yd cream #01
1/2 yd each of greens #32 & 33

white and mauve seed beads

a medium heart Creative Charm

(picture on page 41)

Directions for Flower Garden Heart

1. Transfer stem lines onto print fabric. Stems are one long STRAIGHT stitch made with flower thread. Sew a silk IRIS and FRENCH KNOT, LOOP AND KNOT, and LAZY DAISY flowers and seed beads at the ends of the stem as shown in the diagram.

2. Stitch some pale green leaves, using

Actual Size

JAPANESE stitch, then some dark green leaves that overlap some of them, then stitch more pale green leaves on top. Cut it out, centering the design in the medium heart cutting pattern (page 47). Assemble as directed in charm package.

Ribbon Jewelry

All of the instructions for the delightful collection of silk and French ribbon jewelry pieces pictured on page 40 are included here. With a few silk ribbon embroidery stitches, handmade beads and buttons, you can create a lovely gift. They are so quick and easy, you'll want to make several earrings to go with different outfits. The jacket or dress clip idea will work with a Sunflower, Mum or Daisy as well as the lacy Rose.

There are three styles of earrings on the photo shown. They can be made in many pleasing color combinations, and a variety of fabrics. I have stitched them on silk charmeuse, bridal satins, damask, and regular cotton fabrics. If your fabric is thin, you might want to add a piece of lining, tissue, or same fabric underneath your embroidered fabric to keep the metal dome from shining through.

Our Earring Patterns are created especially for Oh! Donna TM earring parts. These earrings are made to be changed, and can be taken apart several times. Ask for them at your favorite fabric store, or simply use a 1" covered button for the earrings. Different brands of clip on and pierced earring kits are now available at most craft stores.

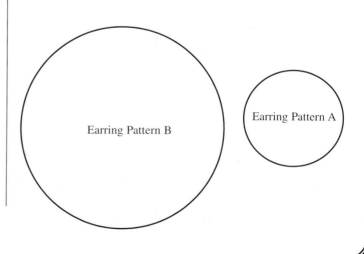

Earring Pattern B

Earring Pattern A

Earrings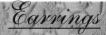

Supply List

1" covered buttons or earring forms

a scrap of fabric, at least 8" X 4" or large enough to go in a 4" embroidery hoop

matching thread

3/8" buttons, seed beads,

embroidery floss green
4MM silk ribbon in the following amounts:
1/2 yd for each woven rose, in your flower color
1 yd green for leaves
1 yd other flower color for daisy
1/2 yd different green for contrast leaves
1 yd of your WOVEN ROSE color for FRENCH KNOTS, or a contrast color

(pictured on page 40)

Directions for Earring

1. Trace two earring circles pattern A (on the previous page) onto your fabric, with a disappearing pen, leaving at least 4" between them. All of the embroidery and beads must be within this circle.

2. Trace the location of the flowers onto the fabric. Use the Silk Ribbon Glossary and diagrams below to see which embroidery stitch to use for which flower, and the color photo to see which colors to use. Work in an embroidery hoop.

3. When the embroidery is finished, sew seed beads on with regular sewing thread as indicated in the diagram. Center the embroidery in the middle of earring pattern B and cut out. Assemble the earrings as directed in package.

Covered Button Broach

Supply List

Dritz® half ball covered button 1½"

size 1" pin back.

pliers
a scrap of fabric large enough to go in the embroidery hoop at least 8" square

6" embroidery hoop

seed beads

1/4" satin twist cord 1/4 yd

4MM silk ribbon in the following amounts:
1/2 yd for rose mauve #163
1/2 yd for bow yellow #14
1 yd dark green #21

1/2 yd *each* of medium green #32
periwinkle #118
grape #85
burgundy #182
light blue #125

(pictured on page 40)

Directions for Broach

1. We used a 1¹/₂" covered button. With a disappearing pen, trace the covered button A pattern (on page 53) onto your fabric. Be sure to leave at least 1" of fabric all around the circle, and enough room to put your fabric in a hoop.

2. Use the diagram to trace the locations of the flowers onto your fabric. Refer to the Silk Ribbon Glossary for how to do silk ribbon embroidery. Work in an embroidery hoop.

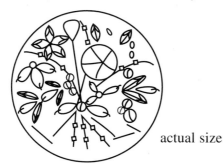

actual size

3. After the embroidery is finished, and beads have been sewn on with regular sewing thread, trim the fabric around your embroidery by placing it in the center of the cover button B pattern, and trimming off the excess fabric.

4. IMPORTANT: Use pliers to remove the button shank from the domed part of the button. Center and stretch fabric over button, hooking fabric onto teeth at opposite sides. Continue to stretch and ease fabric to catch firmly and evenly to teeth all around. Snap on back plate with imprint facing you. Caution, this back is not removable.

5. Glue twist cord around the edge of the cover button. Start by trimming the cord at an angle, and finish by overlapping the ends slightly, and gluing the trimmed finishing end to the back of the beginning end. Use Hot glue to glue a pin back to the back of the broach.

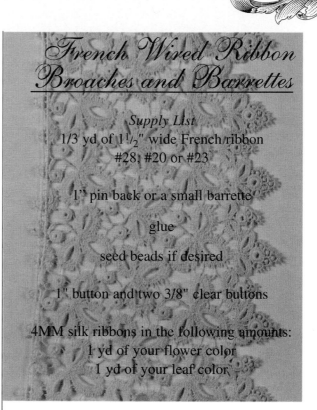

French Wired Ribbon Broaches and Barrettes

Supply List
1/3 yd of 1¹/₂" wide French ribbon
#28, #20 or #23

1" pin back or a small barrette

glue

seed beads if desired

1" button and two 3/8" clear buttons

4MM silk ribbons in the following amounts:
1 yd of your flower color
1 yd of your leaf color

(picture on page 40)
Directions for French Ribbon Broach
These Broaches are made by shirring the French ribbon before embroidering over it with silk ribbons or adding buttons. They also make very fashionable barrette.

1. Cut 12" of ribbon. Turn under both ends of the ribbon 1/4" twice to the wrong side. Fold the ribbon every 2³/₄" to make creases to use for guide lines. Lay the ribbon out flat. Thread the sewing machine with thread that matches one of the darker shades of the ribbon.

2. Starting 1/2" from the dark side of the ribbon, right at the end, machine sew with your longest (basting) straight stitch, to the other end in a wavy line that goes between the dark edge and 1/2" from the dark edge, using the folds to determine where the waves peak. Backstitch, and trim off threads.

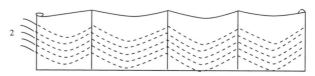

3. Start 1/8" away from your first line of basting and stitch a second row of basting, following the wavy line. Remember to backstitch at the end of each row of basting. Repeat for all 5 rows of stitching.

4. Carefully separate the bobbin threads from the upper threads. Pull the bobbin threads all together to gather the ribbon tightly. Tie off the threads, and tie off the upper threads too.

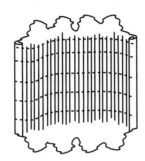

5. Fold the gathered ribbon in half, and sew across both end at an angle as shown. Tie off these threads. Open the broach out flat again. The broach is now ready to embellish. You may glue it to a barrette, a pin back, just plain as it is, or see ideas below for embellishing. If you are going to embellish it, glue the barrette or pin back to it when it is finished.

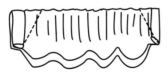

It might be difficult to mark the flower placement onto the ribbon. Try just stitching the flowers first, then add the leaves where they are needed. On the button broach, just sew the buttons in place and add a couple of LAZY DAISY stitches at the sides in silk ribbon.

French Wired Ribbon Jacket or Dress Clip

Supply List
1/8 yd fabric it should coordinate with the rose color

1 yd of 1½" wide French ribbon #30

1/3 yd of flat lace 1¼" wide, (or trim lace if it is too wide)

2 JHB Jacket or dress clips

1/8 yd extra heavy weight interfacing

glue

invisible or matching thread

(pictured on page 40)
Directions for Jacket Clip
(The pattern for Jacket Clip is the same as covered Button B)

1. Cut two jacket clip circles from fabric using pattern on page 53, and two from interfacing.

Prepare the backing by stitching two circles of extra heavy weight interfacing inside of two layers of fabric, that are right side out. Sew all around the outside edge, with a zig zag twice. Trim off frayed threads. Hand or machine sew two jacket clips to the circles as shown. I used the kind with rubber in the gripping edge.

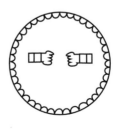

2. Baste 11" of flat lace to the ribbon, starting 9" from the end. This 9" end will be the inside of your wired ribbon Rose, see Wired Rose instructions in the Scattered Flower Collars Chapter of the book. When Rose is finished, glue it to the backing that you prepared.

Lace

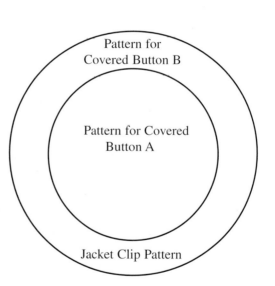

Pattern for
Covered Button B

Pattern for Covered
Button A

Jacket Clip Pattern

Rose Bouquet Stitcher's Handbag ❀ *#203*
Victorian hand bags are decorated by combining Wired Ribbon Roses and dainty silk ribbon stitches, along with delightful buttons and cloth yo yos.

Embellished Accessories

In the past, ladies enjoyed an afternoon of dressing up in their best attire to call on friends. As if they were back in school, everyone took mental notes about every fashion detail and who was wearing the latest styles. The first lady to appear at a social gathering with an intriguing new item created a wave of interest that rippled through every conversation. By the end of the afternoon, all of the ladies would be quietly passing on tidbits about where one might find such elegant accessories.

Today, afternoon teas are once again popular and we are still intrigued by new fashion accessories. In the following pages you will find secrets for making these beautifully embellished accessories.

Instructions for the ribbon work on the two purses pictured at the left are included in this chapter, but don't stop there! Enjoy using a variety of lace medallions, doilies or lace scraps for the background, and add different beaded, metallic gold or braided trims and tassels to the flower nosegay.

An embellished purse would make an exquisite accessory for a special prom or wedding. Embellishments can be glued on to a ready-made purse in no time at all.

Add silk or wired roses to ballet slippers, canvas loafers or soft velvet shoes for a unique and beautiful accessory. A wedding line would be perfect down to the last detail with these comfortable, embellished shoes.

White Shoulder Bag

Supply List
A purchased shoulder bag

1½ yds French ribbon #22

1 pkg seed beads, invisible thread

1 pkg Royal Stitch embroidery wool
color #ew80 or olive green embroidery floss

7MM silk ribbon 1 yd mauve #163

two 3" lace medallions

4MM silk ribbon in the following amounts::
3 yds forest green #21
2 yds med. green #32
2 yds pink #8
1 yd fuchsia #70
1 yd burgundy plum #84
1½ yds grape #85

(pictured on page 54)
Directions for the ribbon work on the white cotton shoulder bag

Position the lace medallions as desired, and machine or hand stitch in place. Mark embroidery placement on top of them. Make a French wired ribbon Rose using one yard of French ribbon color #22 and three Sweet Peas using 5" of the same French ribbon each. Pin these ribbon flowers in place, and trace their shapes with disappearing pen. The wired flowers will be glued or appliqued into place after the embroidery is finished.

Use stitch instructions from the Silk Ribbon Glossary. Refer to the shoulder bag embroidery diagram.

1. Use dark green #21 for all stitches in step #1.
   A. Use the CORAL stitch for the stems.
   B. FLY stitch the plants at the ends of the design.
   C. JAPANESE ribbon stitch the next to the top single stitch of the plants.

2. LOOP stitch three groups of flowers with green #32.

3. The stitches in step 3 are done with burgundy plum #84.
   A. Do TWISTED DAISY flowers along the long stem.
   B. Do FRENCH KNOTS at ends of the main stems, near twisted daisy stitches.

4. Do FRENCH KNOTS between LOOP STITCH rows in Grape color #85.

5. Use mauve ribbon #163 in 7MM width to do FREE FORM TWISTED LOOPS.

6. Use light pink #8 to do: Two clusters of flowers made from LAZY DAISY stitches, then make FRENCH KNOTS and one JAPANESE ribbon stitch on the plants at the very top of the design.

7. Use Fuchsia #70 to make FRENCH KNOTS at your whim inside, and beside the FREE FORM TWISTED LOOPS made in step 5.

8. Use moss green wool #ew80 or embroidery floss to do all of step 8.
   A. Do STRAIGHT stitches in groups of three, near each rose add beads to the end of each stitch.
   B. FLY stitch just above each fly stitch you have done in dark green ribbon on the plants. See step 1B.
   C. FEATHER stitch as marked on diagram and sew a bead at the end of each stitch.

9. Use dark green #21 to do all of step 9.
   A. Do a BULLION tipped lazy daisy stitch
      for the large leaves.
   B. LAZY DAISY stitch one stitch
      over the bottom of the flowers
      sewn in step 6 above. When the
      embroidery is finished, you may
      want to cover the back of the flap
      where all of the knots show. Use
      Wonder Under and the package
      instructions to fuse a piece of the
      purse fabric (the shape of the underside
      of the flap) in place.

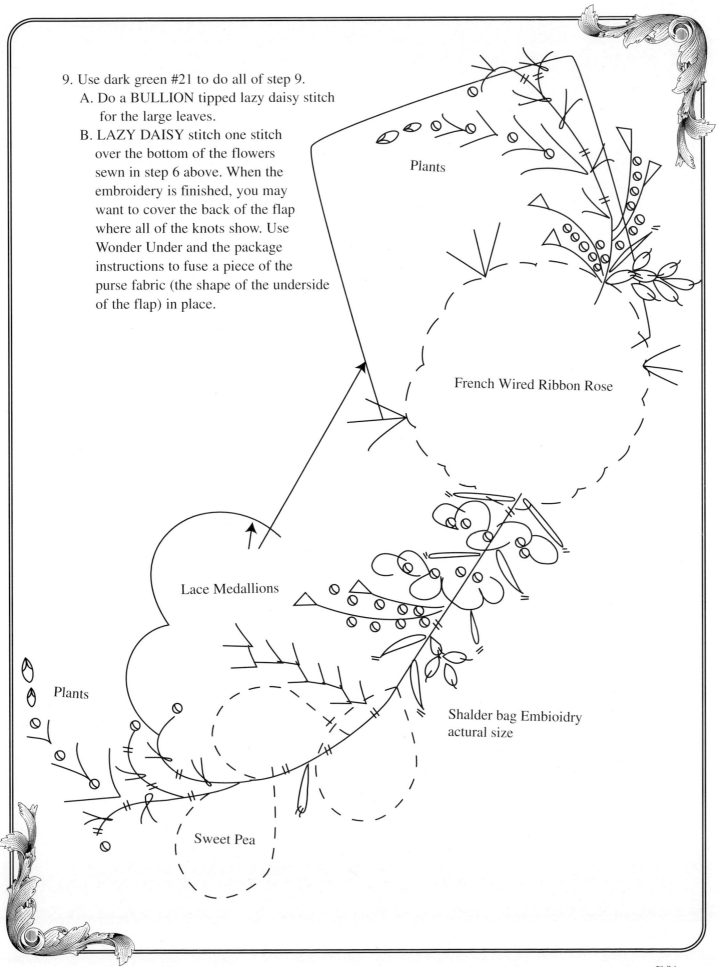

Plants

French Wired Ribbon Rose

Lace Medallions

Plants

Shalder bag Embioidry
acturial size

Sweet Pea

Black Velvet Draw String Handbag

Supply List

A Purchased black velvet bag

6" of 1/2" wide flat lace

6" of French ribbon for Impatiens color #26

One doily or lace medallion
7" X 4" or 6" round

Three buttons

Two scraps of fabric to make yo yos

1 yd French ribbon 1½" wide color #30

1/2 yd green French ribbon color #18

4MM silk ribbon in the following amounts
2 yds green silk ribbon
1/2 yd each of two flower shades

1 pkg seed beads and 6 bugle beads

Invisible thread is optional

Glue

Black Velvet Handbag diagram

(pictured on page 54)

1. Position doily 3" down from the top edge, on the right side, of a velvet purse, and hand tack or glue the doily in place. If you are using an oval, place it on a slant. You may cut the round doily in half, and carefully place the Rose, leaves and yo yo so that they cover the cut edge.

2. Cut two yo yo circles from coordinating fabrics. Use the yo yo pattern and instructions from the bouquet chapter, step E of Daisy. Flatten the yo yo, and when ready. Applique yo yos to the purse front by stitching up through the edge of the yo yo and down through the purse, with little stitches, all around the edge of the yo yo or glue them in place. You will want to finish the Roses and Impatiens before beginning to applique.

3. Make a Wired Ribbon Rose using 27" French 1½" wide ribbon. Make a Rose bud out of 9" of 1½" wide ribbon.

4. Cut green leaf ribbon into three pieces 5" long. Make the leaves using the Folded Leaf instructions from Stem and Leaf chapter.

5. To make a lace flower, sew the two cut ends of the 6" piece of lace together. Gather one edge of the lace into a tight circle. Sew it to the purse with a button, as shown in the picture.

6. Make one Impatiens with the 6" piece of French ribbon.

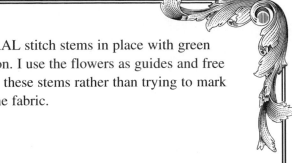

7. Now place the flowers, yo yos and leaves on the doily and mark their placement with a disappearing pen so you will know where to stitch the silk ribbon. Then remove them.

8. Use LAZY DAISY stitch to make three five petal flowers, two are the same color. Use invisible thread to sew three seed beads in the center of each flower.

9. CORAL stitch stems in place with green ribbon. I use the flowers as guides and free hand these stems rather than trying to mark on the fabric.

The ivory drawstring purse pictured at the top is embellished with a ribbon design from the Black Velvet Drawstring Handbag pattern. The other purses are embellished with French Wired Ribbon Roses, Folded leaves, antique buttons and doilies.

Choose any of these three ideas to embellish a purchased shoe:

1. Wired Roses with Gathered leaves made from French ribbon then glued in place.
2. A pansy made from French ribbon and glued onto the shoe.
3. Silk ribbon embroidered rose spray stitched into the shoe.

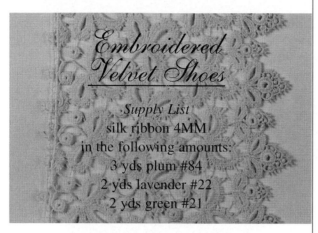

Embroidered Velvet Shoes

Supply List
silk ribbon 4MM
in the following amounts:
3 yds plum #84
2 yds lavender #22
2 yds green #21

(pictured on page 61 top center)
Directions For Embroidered Shoe
Our velvet shoes have an embroidered design on the toe that I use as a guide for the placement of these stitches.

Mark the location of the roses with chalk. You might need a pair of pliers to help pull the needle through. I found that with larger needle sizes, the pliers were not necessary. Glue the ends of the ribbon inside the shoe.

Diagram of embroidery placement

1. Make two dark and one light WOVEN ROSE. Colors #84 dark plum, and #22 lavender.

2. Use green ribbon color #21 to do all of step 2.
   A. Make four leaves with LAZY DAISY stitch above and below the light rose.
   B. Stitch the stem with one long JAPANESE ribbon stitch, and the four leaves that touch it, using the LAZY DAISY stitch.

3. Make two buds with LAZY DAISY stitch on ends of stems with dark plum, and two buds on the very end of the design with lavender.

4. Do small JAPANESE ribbon stitch for leaves on the last bud on the ends of the design.

Embroidery pattern diagram

5. Make a lavender bud with LAZY DAISY stitch, and a FRENCH KNOT tiny bud in front of it, between the two leaves in front.

Ribbon Flowered Slippers #206

Embellished shoes would be delightful for brides or wedding lines. Make your own pair of cloth ballet slippers with pattern 206 (not included). A few silk stitches of any kind can be used to create an original design.

Blossoms On Blouses

A Yellow Pansy

To the wall of the old green garden
A butterfly quivering came;
His wings on the somber lichens
played like a yellow flame.

He looked at the grey geraniums,
And the sleepy four-o'clocks;
He looked at the low lanes bordered
With the glossy-growing box.

He longed for the peace and the
silence,
And the shadows that lengthened
there,
And his wee wild heart was weary
Of skimming the endless air.

And now in the old green garden,—
I know not how it came—
A single pansy is blooming,
Bright as a yellow flame.

And whenever gay gust passes,
It quivers as if with pain,
For the butterfly-soul that is in it
Longs for the winds again!

Helen Gray Cone, 19th Century

Pansy Basket and Rose Trellis Shirts #185

Adorn your own shirt with silk and wired ribbon flowers. These flowers can be used to embellish jumpers or children's clothing. Add the colorful pansy basket to any project for a bright spring look.

Rose Trellis Shirt

Supply List
One 4" crochet doily
Two doilies new or old,
8" diameter to 14" diameter
cloth center is best, but delicate all crochet ones
will do

1/2 yd each of two (1/2" wide) flat narrow laces
1/3 yd of 3" wide flat lace

2 yds French ribbon #19 for leaves

3 $1/3$ yds French ribbon #22 for Roses

1/2 yd 7MM silk ribbon creamy white #01
4MM silk ribbon in the following amounts:
3 yds Dk. green #21
1 yd Md. green #32
4 yds Dk. plum #84
1 yd mauve #163
2 yds grape #85

Mill Hill's seed beads #3036
bugle beads #82009 and assorted
pebble (large) beads
six 3/8" buttons

(pictured on page 62)
Directions for Rose Trellis Shirt
We used two antique doilies. One is an 8"
crochet and the other is a 14" cloth center.
Placement for roses and flower sprays varies,
depending on your doily choice.

1. Put the shirt on a dress form, a friend, or lay the shirt out flat to arrange the doilies on each shoulder. Decide how much of each doily will extend over the shoulder. I cut mine 5 $1/4$" wide. Doily should be 1/4" from the collar seam at the shoulder. Fold the doily on a straight line and press to mark the cutting line, or mark with a disappearing pen. This line might be off center. You may arrange them so more of one doily shows in front and the other doily is more on the back. I have also used heart shaped doilies from Wimpole Street, cut down the center with the rounded part of the heart in front.

Cut the doilies straight across. Pin the doilies to the shirt and pin the wide lace in place connecting the two doilies in the back. Leave 1/2" of wide lace to turn under at both ends, but don't pin the ends down until after step 2.

2. Sew the doilies to the shirt with a close zig zag stitch along the cut edges. Fray check the cut edges.

3. Turn under the ends of the wide lace and sew it in place along the folded ends and top edge. If it is a loose type of lace, zig zag across the ends and fray check them. Pin, then top stitch the narrow lace in place along both edges, covering the cut edges of the doilies. Fold the ends of the narrow lace at an angle if they are not hidden under a Rose.

Make two Roses each from 1 yd of French ribbon, four Buds each from 12" of French ribbon, thirteen Folded leaves. Pin, then mark their placement on the shirt with a disappearing pen. Draw a waving line connecting the Roses over each shoulder, ending behind the Roses on the back. Embroider this stem using the CORAL stitch and green silk ribbon. Remove the Roses and leaves until the embroidery is finished.

Use the flower cluster diagram shown below to embroider silk ribbon flowers on each shoulder. Add buttons and beads to fill in between silk flower

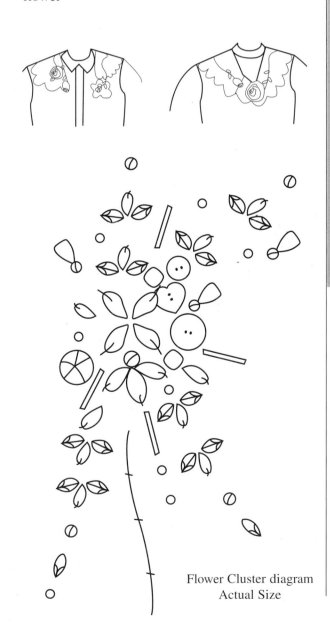

Flower Cluster diagram
Actual Size

Pansy Basket Shirt

See the Supply List at the beginning of this chapter for items that are needed for both shirts

Supply List
8" off white doily
5 yds 4MM medium green #32 silk ribbon (stems)

For Butterfly:
1/6 yd of 1 1/2" wide French ribbon #217
1/2 yd 4MM pink silk ribbon (or embroidery floss) and two pink seed beads

1/3 yd of 1/2" wide flat lace
thread to match

It takes 2/3 yd of French ribbon to make one pansy (21"), and one bud (3"). You need a total of 9 Pansies and five buds. We have used French ribbon color numbers 212, 22, 218, 11, 26, 29, 23, 6, 20 and 217 for our Pansies on various projects.

2 1/6 yds French ribbon for leaves #19

1/2 yd of French ribbon for bow #218

(pictured on page 62)

Directions for Pansy Basket Shirt
1. Use the pattern from the fold out section to cut a basket from a doily. Your doily does not have to be exactly 8" in diameter. Use the outer finished edge of the doily for the top of the basket. Fray check the cut edges of the doily.

Place it on the shirt back, off center. Notice the top edge of the basket is not quite at the center back of the shirt on the picture. Sew over the cut edges of the doily with a close zig zag stitch. Cover the cut edges of the doily with narrow lace. Fold the ends of the lace under 1/2", and fold the lace at an angle at the corners. Stitch on both edges of the lace, and across the top edge of the doily.

2. Make 9 French ribbon Pansies, 5 Buds and 15 Gathered Center leaves, but make a few by pulling the wires in the dark edges. Place them on the shirt to decide where stems should go. Draw stems in place with disappearing pen. You may use the pattern by placing it over the shirt, and push pins through the flower and stem pattern lines and mark where they enter the shirt. (Patterns for the back and front of the Pansy Shirt are found in the fold out section.) Remove the flowers and leaves until the stems are finished. Make the stems using the CORAL stitch. Then glue or applique pansies in place last.

When you applique pansy bud to the shirt, cover the raw ends with a leaf. All of the Pansies, buds and leaves can be glued on. To applique a wired ribbon flower or leaf to a project, use pins to hold it in place. You may use invisible thread or matching thread. When working with invisible thread, use a double thread and a knot in both threads together to keep it from coming unthreaded as you sew.

Also, hide knots on the right side of the shirt, under the edge of the leaf or flower for comfort. Come up from underneath one edge of the flower, and take a small stitch down beside the ribbon into your fabric. Repeat this every 3/8" all around the outside edge of the flower. Then take more stitches through the Pansy, tacking down the edges of all of the petals.

3. Make a butterfly by cutting two wings from pink shaded ribbon using the wing pattern.

Fray check the wings and let them dry. Decide where you want the butterfly, and pin in place. Have the wings touching in the center. Do a satin stitch with floss or silk ribbon for the body. That is, fill in the body with stitches that are right next to each other. Make two long STRAIGHT stitches with a doubled regular sewing thread, for the feelers, and sew beads to the ends. Use matching (regular sewing) or invisible thread and the buttonhole stitch or machine satin stitch to applique the wings to the shirt, all around the outside edge of the wings

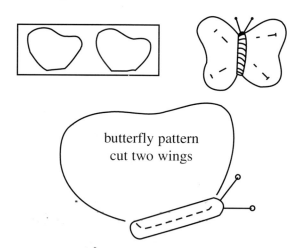

butterfly pattern
cut two wings

BUTTONHOLE STITCH Come up at A, insert at B, and come out at C, taking a small downward stitch, with the thread under the needle. Go in at D and out at E. Continue all around the wings.

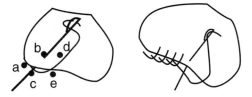

4. Applique a pansy to one cuff, as shown.

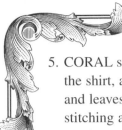

5. CORAL stems for the pansies on the front of the shirt, and applique or glue pansies, buds and leaves to the stems. Stop and tie off stitching at opening edge of shirt front and continue on other side of front.

6. Tie 18" of ribbon in a bow, press it down flat. Pull the wires out of the ends of the ribbon for about 2", and cut the wires off, then smooth out the ribbon. Turn the ends of the ribbon under 1/4". Glue or applique the bow over the pansy stems, either by hand with little blind stitches along the edges, or top stitch along both edges by machine with invisible thread.

Contrasting ribbons make bright pansies on this dark pillow background. Our creamy 1903 Bear #170 sips tea with a vintage Steiff bear.

Portrait of Paradise

What was Paradise?
but a Garden, an
Orchard of Trees and
Herbs, full of
pleasure, and nothing
there but delights...

—William Lawson

When I think of Paradise, I imagine a garden full of roses. On the garden throne reposes the Queen of Flowers, the beautiful red rose, so honored with this title because of its everlasting appeal. It symbolically represents beauty, softness, and love. When someone receives a gift of roses, they are transported for a moment to the garden of paradise.

Although our frame is new, a nice antique frame would be a perfect complement to the ribbon roses. This fast and easy project could be adapted to a variety of frame shapes. The background fabric is natural linen. A silk ribbon rose vine daintily fills the empty space on either side of the glove. Change the vine shape slightly to fit the frame.

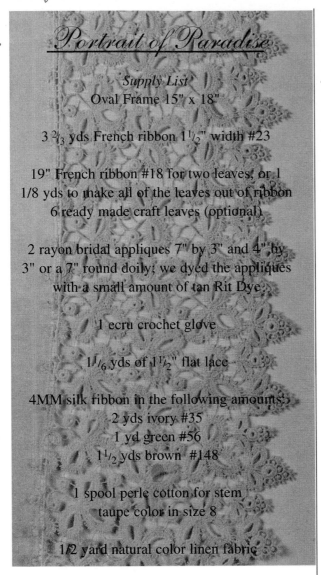

Portrait of Paradise

Supply List
Oval Frame 15" x 18"

3 ⅔ yds French ribbon 1½" width #23

19" French ribbon #18 for two leaves, or 1
1/8 yds to make all of the leaves out of ribbon
6 ready made craft leaves (optional)

2 rayon bridal appliques 7" by 3" and 4" by
3" or a 7" round doily; we dyed the appliques
with a small amount of tan Rit Dye

1 ecru crochet glove

1⅙ yds of 1½" flat lace

4MM silk ribbon in the following amounts:
2 yds ivory #35
1 yd green #56
1½ yds brown #148

1 spool perle cotton for stem
taupe color in size 8

1/2 yard natural color linen fabric

(pictured on page 67)
Directions for Oval Frame

1. Make all of the wired, lace flowers and stems, then arrange them with the glove before marking the embroidery area. Then remove everything and work the embroidery in a hoop. Position the rayon bridal appliques. Then make three Wired Roses, each using 1 yd of ribbon and two buds using 12" of ribbon. One rose and one bud were made by pulling the opposite wired ribbon edge. Two Ivy leaves are made with #18, and we used 6 ready made craft leaves, but it would work beautifully to make all the leaves from ribbon.

2. The lace flower is made by gathering one edge of fine flat cotton lace such as Capitol Imports new lace or a piece of antique lace. Use 1 yard of lace. Include the cut ends of the lace in the gathering, which can be done on the machine or by hand. If sewing by hand, knot the thread and take a few back stitches as you begin, so the knot cannot be pulled through. Gather the lace until it is 12" long. Hold onto one end and coil the lace around itself in a spiral, just as for the Ribbon Rose. The gathered edge is on bottom, the ruffled edge on top. Either hand whip or glue the gathered edge to itself on the underside. Hand tack or glue the lace flower in place. Make a lace bud the same way but use 6" piece of lace.

3. Make a Rolled Wired ribbon stem 9" long, fold it in half and place it across the palm of the glove. The fingers of the glove are folded down completely over the stems, with the thumb crossing over the fingers slightly. One of the wired stems from the artificial leaves is also glued in place under the thumb and index finger.

4. Embroidered vine is made from WOVEN ROSES, LAZY DAISY buds and FRENCH KNOTS made with ivory silk ribbon. Leaves are mixed green and brown JAPANESE ribbon stitch. The green ones have the line down the center. The vines are STEM stitched with perle cotton. Use the diagram in the fold out section. When embroidery is finished, glue the gloves, roses and leaves in place on top of the lace appliques.

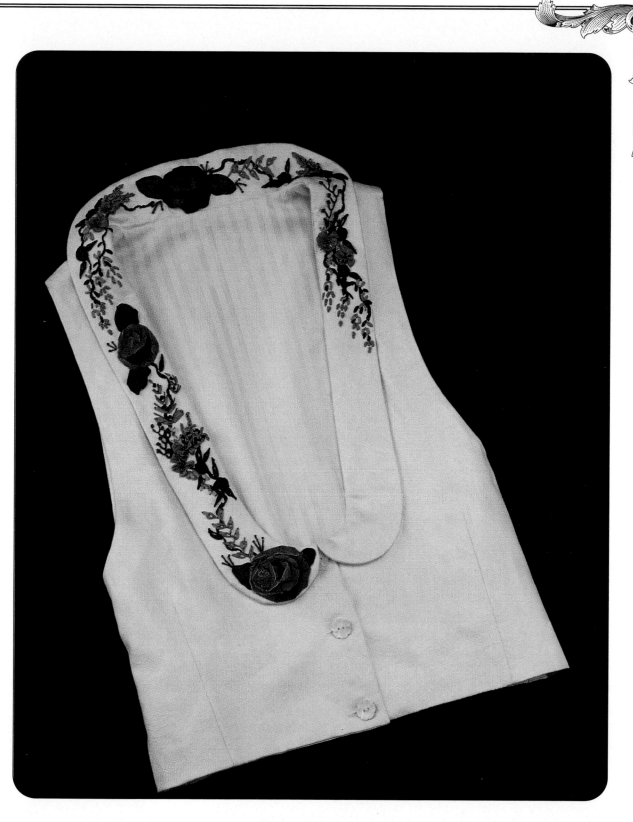

Tuxedo Vest 🌹 *#152*

This slightly fitted tuxedo vest sports several kinds of ribbon flowers. Rich colored silk embroidery combined with dark Wired Roses and leaves make this vest a masterpiece of ribbon work.

Needlework Boxes

During the Victorian era, decorative needlework was called fancy sewing. This was different from plain sewing, which was making or mending clothing. Ladies would often do fancy sewing while paying or receiving calls. An elegant but useful container was needed to carry needlework tools and supplies to the garden, to visit friends, and to attend meetings. "Some women used small pockets or pouches. Others used an étui or small sewing case.

Needlework boxes were considered suitable gifts to celebrate a young woman's engagement, or some other important event in her life."[7]

Four designs for needlework box lids are given here. Any one of them will make your box unique. All of the oval boxes featured in this chapter are from Sudberry House. They have recessed lids which are specially made for needlework.

Shaker Box

Supply List

14" by 14" square of natural linen

2/3 yd of French ribbon #5

1 yd French ribbon #19

1½ yds French ribbon #23

4MM silk ribbon in the following amounts:
3 yds brown #80
2 yds creamy white #01
4 yds green #21
3 yds Med. green #32
2 yds burgundy #182
1 yd Dk. mauve #158
3 yds ivory #34
1 yd copper #148
1/2 yd Lt. pink #8

7MM silk ribbon in the following amounts:
1 yd Dk. rose #114
1/2 yd Med. green #32

Flower Threads in tan #2434,
pale green #2502, brown #2801

(pictured on page 70)

Directions for Shaker Box

It is helpful to make the wired flowers and leaves first, to see how much room to leave for them. (Refer to the Shaker Box diagram on Page 77).

1. Make a Wired Ribbon Rose with 1 yd of French ribbon color #23. Make a Wired Ribbon bud with 12" of French ribbon color #23. Make seven Folded leaves, each using 5" of French ribbon color #19.

2. Top stitch edges of two parallel rows of green French ribbon with matching thread.

3. Arrange and mark placement of rose bud and leaves and draw their stem lines. Stitch stem with CORAL stitch, using copper silk ribbon.

4. STEM stitch stems for all of the small flowers with a single strand of Flower Thread in the colors listed below. Make the silk ribbon flowers and their leaves in the colors indicated below. Refer to the Shaker Box diagram.

   A. WOVEN ROSE and JAPANESE stitch buds are made with burgundy #182 ribbon. Their leaves are green #21 and the stem is tan #2434.

   B. The Gardenia is made by taking 10 long JAPANESE ribbon stitches with white ribbon, radiating out from a center point. Then go around again, adding five slightly shorter JAPANESE ribbon stitches on top of them. The leaves are medium green #32 silk and the stem is pale green #2502. The large JAPANESE stitch leaves are made with #32 silk in 7MM.

   C. The next rose is called LAURA'S ROSE. It has three pale pink #8 STRAIGHT stitches in the center that form a triangle. Then take stitches around it clockwise, with mauve ribbon #158. The bud is three STRAIGHT stitches for the center, and only one more darker ribbon stitch at the base of the bud. The leaves are green #21 and the stem is brown #2801.

D. Daisies are made with three or five STRAIGHT stitches left a little loose with ivory #34, radiating out from a copper #148 FRENCH KNOT center. The leaves are medium green #32 and the stem is pale green #2502.

E. Our large rose is a LAURA'S ROSE done with dark rose #114 7MM ribbon. The creamy rose is a CHAIN STITCH ROSE. Buds are the same ribbon as the rose. The leaves are green #21 and the stem is brown #2801.

F. The CHAIN STITCH ROSE and LAZY DAISY buds are ivory #34. The leaves are medium green #32 and the stem is tan #2434.

G. The last white daisy is 5 LAZY DAISY stitches radiating out from a burgundy FRENCH KNOT. The leaves are green #21 and the stem is brown #2801.

5. Cut a card board oval the same size as the opening in the lid, pad it with quilt batting and glue fabric with stitchery over the batting so there are no wrinkles on the top. Glue the cardboard to the lid of the box.

A mending box is made glorious with ribbon berries, silk roses and sewing tools. These pansies look faded, just like they were pressed in an old album. We used French ribbon colors #51 and #17.

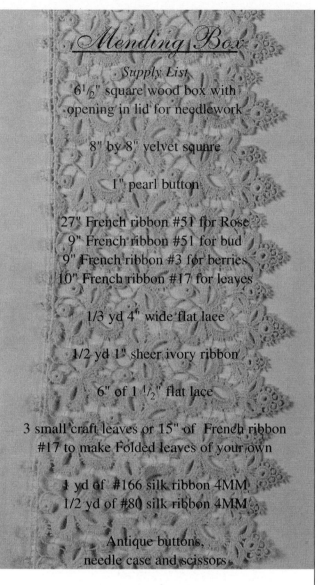

Mending Box

Supply List

6½" square wood box with
opening in lid for needlework

8" by 8" velvet square

1" pearl button

27" French ribbon #51 for Rose
9" French ribbon #51 for bud
9" French ribbon #3 for berries
10" French ribbon #17 for leaves

1/3 yd 4" wide flat lace

1/2 yd 1" sheer ivory ribbon

6" of 1½" flat lace

3 small craft leaves or 15" of French ribbon
#17 to make Folded leaves of your own

1 yd of #166 silk ribbon 4MM
1/2 yd of #80 silk ribbon 4MM

Antique buttons,
needle case and scissors

(pictured on page 72)
Directions for Mending Box

1. Chalk the lid size onto a piece of velvet and add all decorations within the line.

2. Glue 4" lace across velvet at an angle.

3. Sew pearl button on with brown flower thread making the necessary five spokes for a WOVEN ROSE, radiating outward over the edge of the button, from one of the button's holes.

4. Make a WOVEN ROSE from peach silk ribbon by coming up in one of the button's holes. Make two LAZY DAISY buds and a FRENCH KNOT beside the button. Leaves for silk buds are brown JAPANESE ribbon stitches.

5. Make a thimble holder from 1½" lace. Sew it together at the ends, gather the straight edge tightly, and sew or glue it to the background fabric. Baste brown silk ribbon around the top of the lace to tie it.

6. Make a Wired Ribbon Rose using 27" of color #51. Pull the wire in the brown edge.

7. Make a Wired Ribbon Rose bud using 9" of color #51. Pull the wire in the peach edge.

8. Make two Ivy leaves using 5" each of French ribbon color #17.

9. Make three Wired Ribbon Berries from 3" each of French ribbon color #3.

10. Place trio of millinery leaves, antique buttons and a needle package so that they look pleasing with roses, berries and other trimmings. Tack the 1" sheer ribbon to the background fabric (for scissors).

Ribbon Berries

Supply List for Ribbon Berries
3" of French ribbon
for each berry

a small amount of stuffing

matching thread

A. Cut a piece of French ribbon 3" long. Take the wires out of both edges.

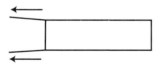

B. Sew or glue the cut ends together using a 1/4" seam allowance.

C. Baste around the bottom edge, pull gathers tight and tie off thread. Baste around top edge.

D. Stuff the berry with a small amount of stuffing. Pull top basting tight and tie off. glue berry in place.

Rose Spray Heirloom Box

Supply List
Ivory linen 6" by 8"

1/2 yd quarter inch satin Ivory twist cord

1 yd ivory sheer ribbon 1" wide

6" piece of 1" wide lace

7MM silk ribbon in the following amounts:
1yd green #72
1/2 yd blue #425
1/2 yd white #01

4MM silk ribbon in the following amounts:
2 yds yellow #14
1/2 yd green #72

2 yds taupe Flower Thread #2611

Seed beads and pearls

Sudberry House's small ivory moire box

(pictured on page 75)
Directions for Rose Spray Heirloom Box
The Rose Spray Heirloom Box is made to be used on Sudberry House's small moire box.

1. Transfer diagram 1 from page 76 to the linen. Use a disappearing pen. Trace the stem line, mark dots for beginning of FEATHER stitches, flowers location, and FRENCH KNOTS.

2. With STEM stitch, stitch the curved stem line with one strand of Flower Thread.

3. Use FEATHER stitch to stitch vines below the flowers, with one strand of Flower Thread.

4. Make a yellow WOVEN ROSE at X. Do three LAZY DAISY buds above it, and one at the top of the flower spray.

5. Use JAPANESE stitch, and wide blue ribbon to make the large flower and buds.

6. Use white ribbon to make FRENCH KNOTS at the symbol that looks like a circle with two lines going through it. Use yellow ribbon to make them at the regular FRENCH KNOT symbol.

7. Use wide green to make JAPANESE stitch leaves around the blue flowers.

8. Mix narrow green and yellow JAPANESE stitch buds and leaves at random on the feather stitch vines. Sew seed beads at the ends of the remaining feather stitches. Sew seed beads and pearls between the FRENCH KNOTS on the stem, with regular sewing thread. Sew seed beads near the ends of the stem too.

9. Sew the ends of the lace together and gather the straight edge by basting along it, and pulling the basting thread tightly. Tie off thread, and wrap it around the middle of the lace forming a bow shape. Set it aside and tie a bow in the middle of the ribbon, and tack the bow and lace to the linen just above the stitchery. Twist the ends of the bow close around the stitchery, and tack them down each time the ribbon twists with a seed bead.

10. Cut out a cardboard oval the size of diagram 1. Pad it with a small scrap of quilt batting. Trim away excess linen 1 $^1/_2$" from oval line in. Wrap stitchery over batting, and glue it to the underside. Glue lid in place on box lid, and glue twist cord around the edge of the stitchery, overlapping ends under the bow.

Rose Spray Heirloom Box and Green Rose Box

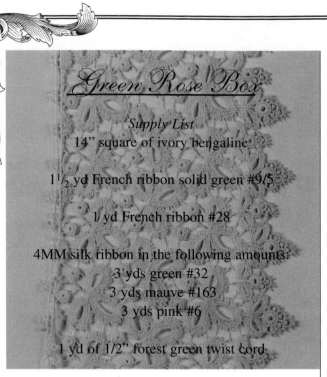

Green Rose Box

Supply List
14" square of ivory bengaline

1½ yd French ribbon solid green #9/5

1/ yd French ribbon #28

4MM silk ribbon in the following amounts:
3 yds green #32
3 yds mauve #163
3 yds pink #6

1 yd of 1/2" forest green twist cord

(pictured on page 75)

One French Wired Ribbon Rose, petite silk stitches, and graceful sheer ribbon can be combined on the tops of modest boxes to bring out their glory and ability to decorate a corner.

Two Ivy leaves made from sheer emerald ribbon accent the Wired Ribbon Rose on this green Moire box, by Sudberry House. A forest green French ribbon is twisted around the lid, with simple silk ribbon LAZY DAISY buds in two shades of mauve holding it down. Leaves for the buds are JAPANESE ribbon stitch in a medium green silk. The ribbon work is done on an ivory moire fabric, then glued over batting and a card board lid insert. A wired bow and twist cord are glued on last.

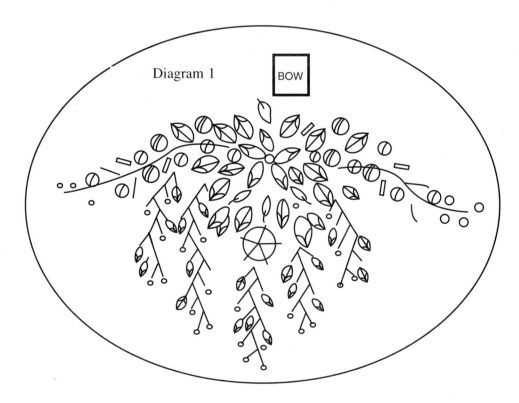

Rose Spray Heirloom Box Diagram
actual size

Shaker Box Diagram Actual Size

Spring Flower Collection

$\mathcal{W}$hat season is more longed for, antici-
pated and gladly welcomed than spring? At our
home in the mountains, we know that winter is
fading when the little green shoots of the daffodils bravely raise their heads through the last
traces of snow. Although sometimes the sprouts
disappear under a fresh blanket of snow, the
daffodils are always victorious, bringing their
sunny brightness to the garden in the end.
Spring flowers are my favorites because they
come at a time when the landscape looks so
dreary. Though they are small, they make such
a difference!

The attractive spring flowers collection includes
instructions on how to make the Tulip, Daffodil
and Jonquil out of French Ribbons. These
delightful bulb flowers can be made short or tall
and in a variety of colors. Each flower could
add its own spring flavor to the hem of a denim
shirt. They will also make a year round colorful
center piece for any battenburg or solid colored
tablecloth. Try them on a child's romper, over-
alls or jacket. The flowers can also be
arranged as shown here to add color and appeal
to our pleated jumper. Sunflowers are made
using the Daisy instructions in the Bouquet
chapter.

Spring Flower Jumper 🌹 *#213*

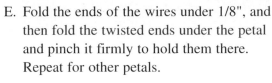

E. Fold the ends of the wires under 1/8", and then fold the twisted ends under the petal and pinch it firmly to hold them there. Repeat for other petals.

Daffodil

Supply List for one Daffodil
29" of yellow
French Wired Ribbon #11

1 yd 7MM green silk
for leaf and stem

Matching thread

A. Cut 5 yellow petals 5" long from French ribbon.

B. Fold the ribbon in half. Fold the folded edge down again at a right angle, crease this fold, then unfold it and sew along the crease line.

C. Open the petal out flat, and hide the folded edge underneath.

D. Bunch up the cut ends, and twist them together.

F. Top stitch a stem of 7MM silk ribbon in place. Place petals in a circle at the top of the stem. Sew around the outside edges to tack the petals in place, or use glue around the underside edge, and press gently in place.

G. Cut a piece of ribbon 4" long, fold it in half, and sew a 1/4" seam across the cut ends. Push back on the ribbon and expose both of the wires in one edge. Pull them both at the same time, until about 1" of wire is out of the ribbon. Twist it together and cut off half of it. Fold the remaining wire under twice, and repeat for the wires in the other edge of the ribbon.

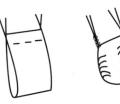

H. Adjust the gathers around the circle, flatten it and glue or sew in place on top of the 5 petals as shown, so the seam is hidden underneath. Daffodil leaves are made by using the Silk Bulb Leaf from the stem and leaf chapter.

Tulips

Jonquils

Supply List for one Tulip
15" French ribbon
#217 for flower

Use the Daffodil petal directions A through E to make three petals out of French ribbon for your Tulip. Layer them as shown, and stitch or glue in place. Make leaves by using the Wired Bulb leaf instructions from the Stem and Leaf chapter. The stem can be made from the Rolled Ribbon stem or a matching 7MM silk ribbon that is top stitched down the center of the ribbon.

A tulip pillow trimmed with vintage lace makes every picnic perfect. Old table linens form a lacy background for the bright French ribbon tulips.

Supply List for one Jonquil
15" French ribbon in yellow #11 or white
1 yd of green 7MM silk for leaves and stem
4" French ribbon #181 for jonquil center

A. Make three petals from yellow or white wired ribbon, using the Daffodil petal instructions A through E.

B. Tie a knot in the 4" piece of peach French ribbon, and fold the ends under 1/4" twice, together, and glue or sew the knot at the center of the petals. Use the Silk Bulb Leaves.

A Garden of Flowers

The wall hanging pictured right, is a sampler composed of various wired ribbon flower designs. Instructions for all of the flowers on the sampler have been included in this book.

The flowers appear in this order from the ornament at the top to the bottom: Cocarde, Sweet Peas, Morning Glory, Impatiens, Pansy and Roses. The instructions for the Cocarde and Impatiens are included here, and the other flower instructions are found by looking in the Table of Contents.

Here you'll learn to make a little tuft of a flower we call the impatiens. This unassuming little flower will become a favorite because it is so quick and easy to make. Think of the impatiens whenever a small, bright bouquet filler is needed. The impatiens pictured are made from a rayon ribbon that is shaded along the length of the ribbon. If this ribbon is difficult to find, use our directions for French Ribbon Impatiens. These impatiens are shown on the front cover.

French Cocardes were used on hats, belts and purses. Cocarde means rosette in French and resembles a ribbon daisy.

Flower Garden Sampler #204

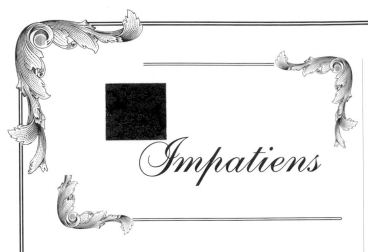

Impatiens

Freshen up an old gardening hat with Morning Glories that trail over the brim. A Cocarde and two Wired Ribbon Roses embellish the other straw hat. They are perfect accessories for a tea party or a day in the garden.

*Supply List to make five blooms
on the stem as show on the sampler*

30" of French ribbon #212,
or 6" per bloom

1/2 yd of French ribbon #186
for stem and leaf

A. To make one blossom cut a piece of French ribbon 6" long.

B. Sew the ends of one 6" ribbon together, using a 1/4" seam allowance.

C. Gather the flower by basting down the center and pulling the gathering thread tightly. Fold the flower in half so the two ruffled edges are on top, and the gathered fold is then sewn to the background fabric, on the stem. Repeat for other blooms as desired.

D. To make a flower spray like the one on the wall hanging, make a Rolled stem from 8" of French ribbon and two Folded leaves.

E. Arrange and glue the flowers and leaves in a pleasing way along the stem.

Cocarde

Supply List for one Cocarde
1 2/3 yds French ribbon #22
1" button optional

A. Fold dark edge of ribbon down, leaving a 1/2" tail.

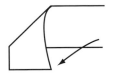

B. Fold ribbon into a point, then fold right side over on top of the left side.

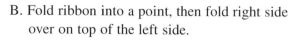

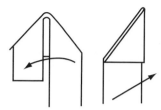

C. Fold ribbon to make a new point at the left side, and fold it up on top of first point.

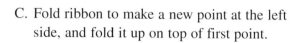

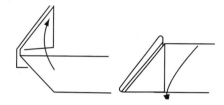

D. Make a new point at the top as in step B. Fold the right side over on top of the left side. Continue making points and folding them over until you have 26 dark points.

E. Make a ring with the ribbon by sewing the two little raw ends together with a needle and thread. Hand sew the light points together by sewing through the very end of each point, and drawing the thread up as tight as it will go. Tie off the thread.

F. Walk your thumbs around the circle, pushing the dark points over to one side so it looks like a pin wheel. Then fold every other point in half so the dark point touches the light point at the center. Sew a button to the center

Glossary Of Silk Ribbon Stitches

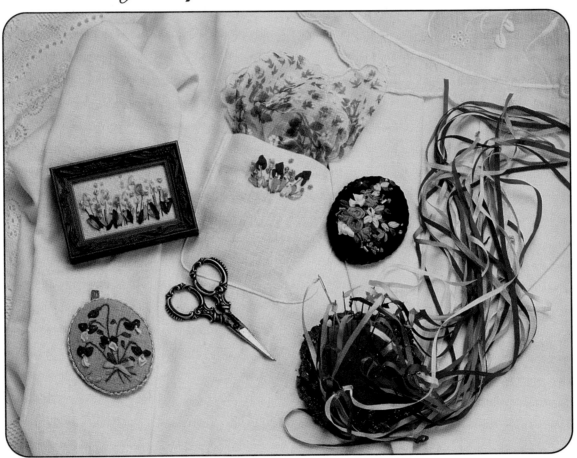

The silk IRIS design is a delicate addition to this white linen jacket, and it makes a cute gift stitched in a tiny frame. (See the Victorian Jewelry chapter for pattern)

When choosing needles for silk ribbon embroidery, consider the weave of the fabric. A needle with a fine but long eye will do nicely for the usual 4MM and 7MM silk ribbons, if your background fabric is thin, light weight or loosely woven. A larger long eye will save wear and tear on the silk if it is being pulled through a heavier weight fabric like denim, or layers of velvet crazy quilt. A nice supply of chenille and crewel needles in assorted sizes is useful. My favorites are sizes 18-22. Avoid tapestry needles, because they have a blunt point. When working on an embroidery project, thread a separate needle with each new ribbon color. My needles sit in a pincushion like so many little medieval banners, waiting until I need that color again.

It is easier than trying to unlock the ribbon from the eye of the needle to rethread it every time I want to use a new color. I have purchased several packages of my favorite sizes, and usually have at least 25 banners in my cushion.

Ester's Needles by YLI corp. are a collection of every needle you would need for silk ribbon embroidery. It is a great way to start, and thenn you can add more of your favorite sizes. You will need beading needles to sew on some kinds of seed beads. I like the Mill Hill brand beads because they have a large enough hole that they can usually be sewn on with my regular sharps.

General Embroidery Instructions

When working with silk ribbon, the methods are similar to those used when embroidering with floss (except the knots) and needle threading, which are explained below. Use 18" lengths of ribbon. Let the ribbon remain slightly loose in your stitches. If you pull it tight or let it twist, it will look like regular floss. Always use 4MM silk ribbon unless otherwise instructed.

KNOTTING INSTRUCTIONS

A. Thread the needle, then sew through the short end of the ribbon. Pull on the long end of the ribbon until the short end tightens up in the eye of the needle.

B. For the knot at the end of the ribbon, make a little fold at the end of the long ribbon and sew through it, holding onto the fold until all the ribbon has passed through it.

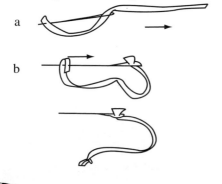

At the end of a stitched design, a regular knot will do, It would also be wise to work in a hoop whenever possible. If the project has a combination of wired and silk ribbon flowers on it, make the wired ribbon flowers and leaves first to see how much room they will need. Pin these ribbon flowers in place, and trace their shapes with a disappearing pen. Then do all of the silk ribbon embroidery before attaching the wired flowers. Usually, wired flowers are thick and get in the way of the embroidery hoop.

SILK RIBBON STITCHES

The symbol for each of the silk ribbon stitches or flower is next to the name of the stitch. These symbols will be found throughout the book in several of the diagrams and illustrations of stitch combinations. Refer to this section to see which stitch matches with each symbol shown in your particular project.

BULLION TIPPED LAZY DAISY

Make a single bullion lazy daisy stitch by coming up at A, go back in at A and up at B, and wrap the ribbon around the point of the needle three times. Pull gently on the ribbon. Hold the wraps snugly down on the fabric with the thumb, and pull the needle through, then go into the fabric at C.

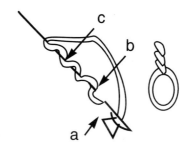

CHAIN STITCH ROSE

Come up at A, insert the needle at A, and come up at B, and wrap the ribbon around the point of the needle. Pull the needle through, and stitch into the fabric at B and come up at C. Wrap the ribbon around the point of the needle and pull it through. Repeat, working around in a circle. Usually about 11 stitches make a nice rose. You may also work about 7 chain stitches to form a circle around FRENCH KNOTS beads, or three straight stitches. Join the last chain to the first using a STRAIGHT stitch.

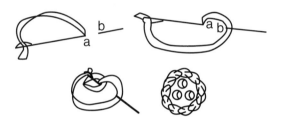

CORAL STITCH STEM

Come up at A. With the ribbon held along the stitching line with your thumb, and the ribbon forming a circle over your thumb, take a tiny stitch under the ribbon and come up into the circle. Pull until it forms a tiny knot. Repeat until you come to the end of the stem line, then stitch to the back of the fabric, knot the ribbon, or glue the end of the ribbon.

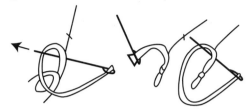

FEATHER STITCH

Bring the needle out at the top center A. Hold the thread down with the left thumb, insert the needle at B on the same level, and come out at C (half way between A and B, and a little lower), with the thread under the needle. Then insert the needle at D, on the same level as C, and come out at E (halfway between C and D, and a little lower), with the thread under the needle. Continue to the end then just take a STRAIGHT stitch to hold the last stitch in place.

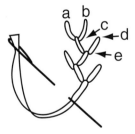

COUCHED STEMS

Come up at the place you want to begin the stem. Lay the ribbon out flat, along the drawn stem line. Sew through the fabric at the end of the line. Leave the ribbon loose, with at least a 4" tail on the backside. With regular thread, ribbon or even another shade of ribbon, come up from underneath, on the stem line, and take a tiny stitch over the first ribbon, every half or quarter inch, to hold it in place. Knot ends on the back.

FLY STITCH

Bring the ribbon through at A, hold it down with the left thumb. Insert the needle at B, and come out at C, with the ribbon under the needle. Take a tiny stitch into the fabric over the ribbon at C.

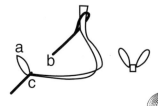

FREE FORM TWISTED LOOPS

This stitch is worked like the LOOP stitch, except you will twist the ribbon once before inserting the needle at B. When you come up through the ribbon sew through the flat part of the ribbon. Be careful to not sew through the knot used to begin the stitch, because it will pull out the first loop. Use a needle or tooth pick to hold the previous loop while making the next stitch.

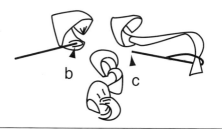

FRENCH KNOT

Bring the needle up at A and pull the ribbon through. Wrap the ribbon around the needle twice, near where the ribbon comes out of the fabric. Hold the wraps gently, and stitch down next to A, but don't pull the stitch too tight.

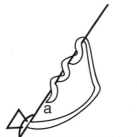

GATHERED ROSE

Come up through the fabric with 7MM ribbon. With a regular needle, and matching thread, baste one edge of the 7MM ribbon for 2". Pull up the gathering thread, and coil the gathered ribbon around itself. Sew to the back side with the gathering thread, then come up and stitch through the bottom of the flower to hold it in the coil. Tie off the thread on the back side. Sew through the fabric and knot the ribbon.

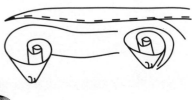

IRIS

Make a LAZY DAISY stitch at the end of the stem, and then come out of the fabric below the bud and slide the needle through the stitch. Then go back through the fabric at the other side of the stem.

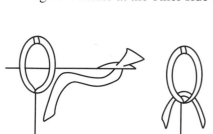

Green

JAPANESE RIBBON STITCH

Come up at A, and stitch down through the ribbon at B. Stop pulling when the ends of the ribbon curl up.

JAPANESE FLOWER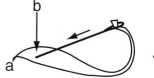

Make three overlapping JAPANESE ribbon stitch petals. One type of Japanese flower is made by making three or four JAPANESE stitches in a circle or half circle.

LAURA'S ROSE

Make three STRAIGHT stitches in the center, using pale ribbon, that form a triangle. Then take stitches around it clockwise, with darker ribbon, overlapping the ends of the stitches before, until the Rose is big enough. The bud is the three STRAIGHT stitches for the center, and only one more darker ribbon stitch at the base of the bud.

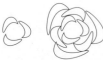

87

LAZY DAISY BUD
LAZY DAISY LEAF Green

Come up at A. Insert the needle at A and come up at B, and wrap the ribbon around the point of the needle. Pull the needle through and stitch over the ribbon at B.

LOOP AND KNOT FLOWER

Come up at A, go in at B, slightly in front of A. Come up through the ribbon near B. Go back into the fabric at C. Come up through the ribbon at C, and make a FRENCH KNOT.

LOOP STITCH

Start by coming up at the top, A, and working down. Insert the needle into the fabric at B. Hold this loop at the desired length with a large needle or tooth pick. While holding the loop flat on the fabric, stitch up through the ribbon just above B. Pull the stitch tight.

Hold this new loop with the tooth pick, and insert the needle at C. Come up through the ribbon above C and proceed as before until the last stitch, which can be a STRAIGHT stitch, just to hold the last loop in place. I like to make two rows of loops meet at an angle at the bottom.

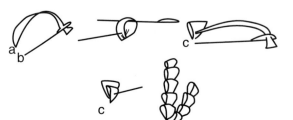

SILK RIBBON PANSY ×

Stitch two LAZY DAISY leaves with 7MM green ribbon. Stitch two LAZY DAISY petals with a darker colored 7MM ribbon. Stitch three LAZY DAISY petals in lighter 4MM ribbon, with two of the petals overlapping the two darker petals, and a FRENCH KNOT from darker ribbon in the middle.

STEM STITCH

Come up at A, go in at B, and up at C, keeping the working ribbon underneath.

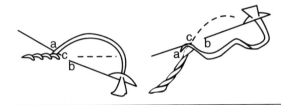

STRAIGHT STITCH /
A simple straight stitch.

TWISTED DAISY ⌄

Come up at A, insert the needle at B, and come up at C. Wrap the ribbon under the needle as shown, then pull the needle out and go over the ribbon at C with a tiny stitch.

WOVEN ROSE ⊗

With regular thread, stitch five stitches meeting in the center of a circle 3/8" across. Come up with the ribbon near the center of the circle, and weave it over and under each spoke of the circle. Let the ribbon twist. When the spokes are full, knot the ribbon on the back.

Antique laces remind us of an era when even unseen trimmings were exquisite and feminine. Here we have added silk embroidery to vintage lace. The rare drizzling kit from the early nineteenth century contains needle work tools that are displayed in their original French case with a lithograph cover.

Stems And Leaves

Stems

CORAL STITCHED STEM

This can be stitched with either 4MM or 7MM silk ribbon. Leaves are made for this stem by using the silk ribbon to do LAZY DAISY stitches or add wired ribbon leaves. I especially like the effect of the CORAL stitched stem with Wired Roses. The little stitch over the ribbon every 1/2" reminds me of thorns. It looks like couching, but is easier because you are only working with one needle and one piece of ribbon. Try threading two colors of silk ribbon in your needle at once, for a variegated appearance. See CORAL stitch on page 86.

COUCHED STEMS

This is a nice way to do stems where two ribbon colors are desirable. You can couch with a different color than the stem and produce an interesting shaded appearance. Try using two different shades of green or tan, in two separate needles. Or COUCH over two ribbons of similar shades, which are twisted sometimes showing the lighter shade and sometimes the darker one. See COUCHED stems on page 86.

ROLLED WIRED RIBBON STEMS

Cut a piece of green shaded wired ribbon as long as you would like the finished stem to be plus an extra half of an inch. Turn under both raw ends 1/4" to the same side. Fold the

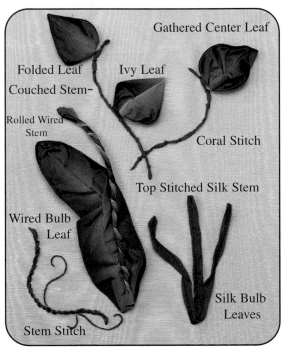

Here are five different ways to portray flower stems and leaves.

ribbon in half lengthwise with the ends inside. Twist the ribbon tightly. Glue or pin ribbon in place, or blind stitch stem by coming up from underneath with matching thread, and taking a tiny stitch in a twist where it will not show, for the entire length of the stem.

STEM STITCH

This stitch can be worked with Flower Thread, perle cotton or silk ribbon in 4MM or 7MM. It looks nice worked with Flower Thread for stems in delicate flower clusters. When using silk ribbon, this stitch gives a rope-like effect to the stem. It also looks nice when used for a dainty basket handle. STEM stitch is on page 88.

TOP STITCHED SILK STEM

Make a stitch the length of the flower stem with 7MM silk ribbon. Top stitch down the center by machine with matching thread. A second way to do this stem is to lay a length of ribbon on the design, if a seam will cover the lower raw edge and the blossom will cover the upper edge, and top stitch down the center by machine.

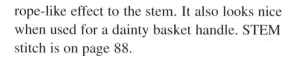

Leaves

FOLDED LEAF

A. Cut shaded green French ribbon 5" long, or 6" for $1^1/_2$" wide ribbon.

B. Fold the ribbon in half. Fold the folded edge down again at a right angle, crease this fold, then unfold it, and sew or glue along the crease line. When the ribbon is shaded from light to dark green, using a different side of the same ribbon makes a leaf of a different shade.

C. Open the leaf out flat, and hide the folded edge underneath.

D. Bunch up the cut ends, and twist them together while holding the leaf with your other thumb and index finger.

E. Fold the ends of the wires under 1/8", and then fold the twisted ends under the leaf and pinch it firmly to hold them there, or hide the twisted ends under a flower.

F. Sew around the outside edges to tack the leaves in place, or use glue around the underside edge, and press gently in place. Some of the French ribbons have one edge that is green, and the other edge is a flower color. It makes an interesting combination to make the flower out of the color and the leaf out of the green edge.

IVY LEAVES

I usually make Ivy Leaves from a 5" piece of ribbon, but use a shorter or longer piece depending on the size that you want the leaf to be.

A. Hold the ribbon with the lighter edge on top, and fold both ends of the ribbon down at a right angle, with one in front, and one in back as shown.

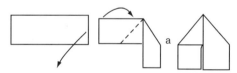

B. Hold the leaf in your thumb and index finger as shown, and twist the ends together.

C. Fold the ends under and pinch them firmly to keep them there. Glue or applique each leaf in place now by stitching just over the outer wired edges with tiny stitches and matching thread. Stitch a row of stitching down the center of each leaf, or glue it on the back side.

GATHERED CENTER LEAF

A. Cut a piece of French ribbon 5" long. Fold the ribbon in half and gently push the ribbon back from the wires in the light side, then pull on both wires at the same time. Pull them as tight as you can without breaking the wires. Then twist them together so they will not come undone.

B. Scrunch and twist, or baste the cut ends together. Fold the raw ends under, or hide the raw ends under a flower.

WIRED BULB LEAF

This leaf is excellent for the Tulip, Iris, or any other bulb type flower that requires a wide leaf.

A. Cut French ribbon twice as long as you would like the finished leaf to be, plus one inch. Fold it in half. On the machine, sew each ribbon as shown. Begin sewing near the folded edge. The leaf will be mostly the color of the edge where you begin sewing.

B. Fold the corner down twice. Open the leaf out flat, and twist the cut ends together, and hide the ends behind the leaf, or hide the raw ends in a seam.

C. Bend little folds in the leaves if desired, and applique or glue the leaf in place.

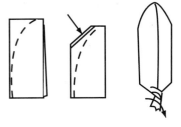

SILK BULB LEAF

These are made with one long stitch each, using 7MM silk ribbon and a needle.

A. Begin the stitch near the lower edge of the top stitched silk flower stem, and enter the fabric near the petals, or to the side of the stem. Allow the ribbon to twist once.

B. When leaves are in place, top stitch down the center of each leaf with a machine stitch, and matching thread, back stitching a few stitches at the ends of the leaves.

a   b

French Ribbon Chart

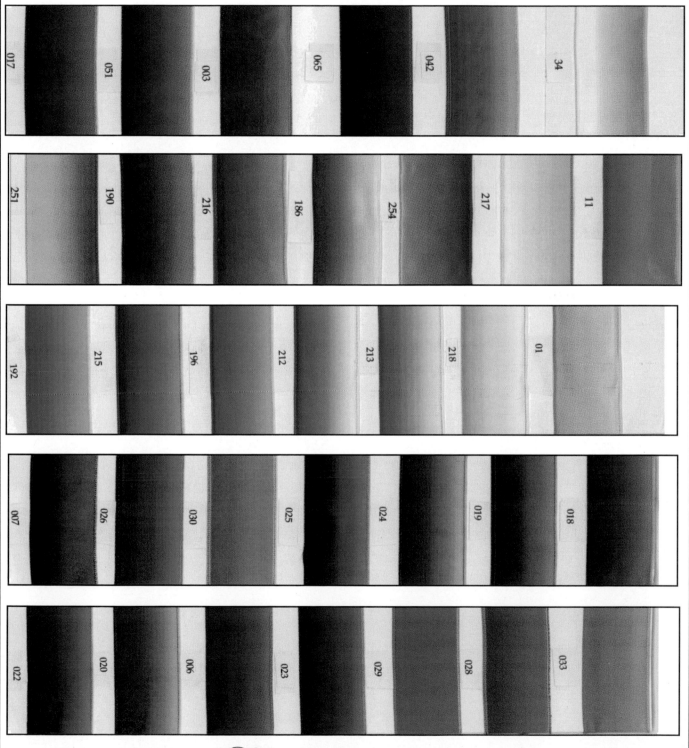

017 051 003 065 042 34

251 190 216 186 254 217 11

192 215 196 212 213 218 01

007 026 030 025 024 019 018

022 020 006 023 029 028 033

Shades may vary

Important Contributors

We would like to thank. Sudberry House for the Moire Boxes. We appreciate the beautiful buttons from the JHB button company. Capitol Imports supplied many of the antique-looking fine laces. Vaban Ribbons International donated many beautiful French ribbons for our samples. We appreciate their generosity and help with all of our questions.

My Gratitude to these inspiring artists —

I want to give a special heartfelt thanks to Elly Sienkiewicz who taught me how to make the wired ribbon Roses, and allowed me to use the idea. From that moment my designs took a new direction. I am deeply indebted to Judith Montano who opened my eyes to silk ribbon possibilities.

Kathy Pace, 1995

Bibliography

Page numbers refer to the books listed below

Anderson, Kay. <u>Fashion With Ribbon</u>, Tiptree, Essex: Anchor Brendon Ltd, 1987.
Footnote #1, Page 9. Footnote #3, page 8. Footnote #5, page 9. Footnote #6, page 9.

Bawden, Judith. <u>The Hat Book</u>: Creating Hats For Every Occasion, Ashville, NC: by Lark Books, 1993.
Footnote #2, page 11. Footnote #4, page 10.

Rogers, Gay Ann. <u>An Illustrated History of Needlework Tools</u>, Brattleboro, VT: by The Book Press, 1983
Footnote #7, page 21.

About the Author

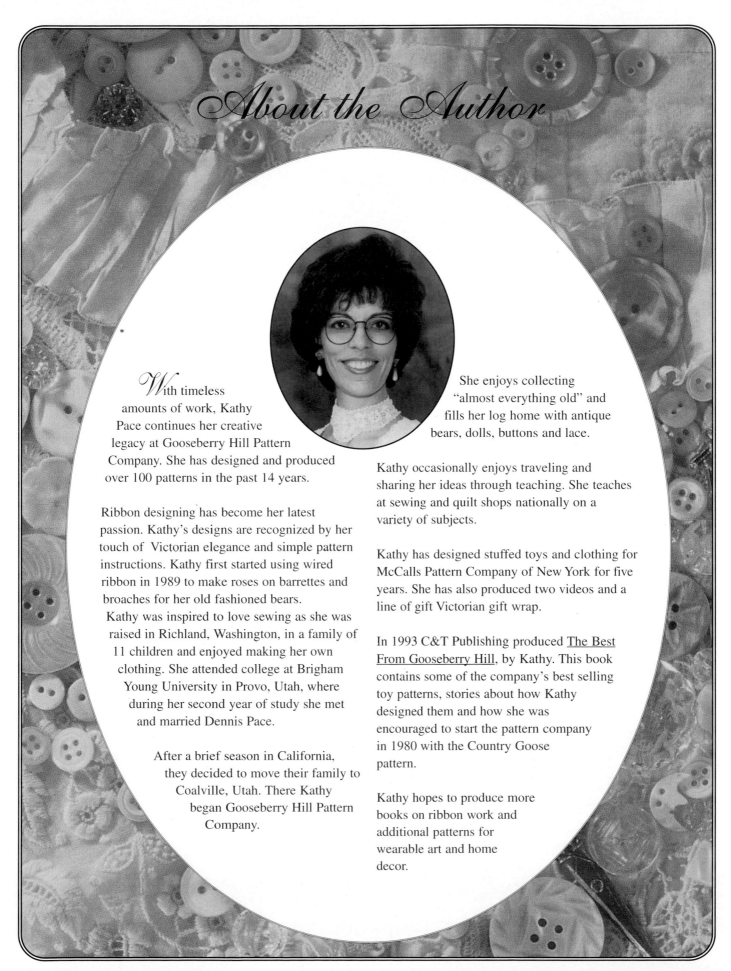

*W*ith timeless amounts of work, Kathy Pace continues her creative legacy at Gooseberry Hill Pattern Company. She has designed and produced over 100 patterns in the past 14 years.

Ribbon designing has become her latest passion. Kathy's designs are recognized by her touch of Victorian elegance and simple pattern instructions. Kathy first started using wired ribbon in 1989 to make roses on barrettes and broaches for her old fashioned bears.
Kathy was inspired to love sewing as she was raised in Richland, Washington, in a family of 11 children and enjoyed making her own clothing. She attended college at Brigham Young University in Provo, Utah, where during her second year of study she met and married Dennis Pace.

After a brief season in California, they decided to move their family to Coalville, Utah. There Kathy began Gooseberry Hill Pattern Company.

She enjoys collecting "almost everything old" and fills her log home with antique bears, dolls, buttons and lace.

Kathy occasionally enjoys traveling and sharing her ideas through teaching. She teaches at sewing and quilt shops nationally on a variety of subjects.

Kathy has designed stuffed toys and clothing for McCalls Pattern Company of New York for five years. She has also produced two videos and a line of gift Victorian gift wrap.

In 1993 C&T Publishing produced <u>The Best From Gooseberry Hill</u>, by Kathy. This book contains some of the company's best selling toy patterns, stories about how Kathy designed them and how she was encouraged to start the pattern company in 1980 with the Country Goose pattern.

Kathy hopes to produce more books on ribbon work and additional patterns for wearable art and home decor.

Other Fine Products Available From Gooseberry Hill

A Ribbon Bouquet Video
A companion to A Ribbon Bouquet book: In this exciting program, you will see how easy it is to make a variety of beautiful French ribbon flowers, leaves and stems.

A variety of beautiful patterns for clothing and home decor

French wired ribbons

Silk ribbons

Crochet collars and gloves

Teddy bear supplies, including European mohair, and our instructional video, Heirloom Bears.

Gift wraps (#100 is pictured on page 95)

The Best of Gooseberry Hill a book by Kathy Pace

Ask for Gooseberry Hill's products at your favorite fabric shop or call (801) 336-2116 for more information. Wholesale inquiries call (801) 336-2780
Gooseberry Hill
1881 Old Lincoln Highway
Coalville, Utah 84017